Gabor Baross:

HUNGARY AND HITLER

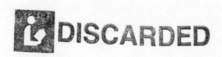

Problems Behind the Iron Curtain Series No. 8

Hungary and Hitler

by *Gabor Baross*

Former member of the Hungarian Parliament

*Reprinted from the Living History Program of the
University of Southern California
with the permission of the Author and the University.*

Library of Congress Catalog Card Number: 79-130638

PPROBLEMS BEHIND THE IRON CURTAIN SERIES:

The Sovereign Press, 52 McCaul Street, Toronto, Canada

HUNGARY AND HITLER

The average foreigner does not know Hungarian history in detail and does not know the Hungarian people. To be able to understand the relationship that developed between Hungary and Hitler's Third Reich which led to the tragedy of the Hungarian nation, it is essential that one becomes cognizant of the following historical facts and bears them in mind for the duration of the study.

From the moment the Hungarians took over the heritage of their ancestors in the Carpathian basin (at the end of the tenth century A.D.) they battled constantly with the German imperialistic trends known to science as "Drang Nach Osten" [in English: Urge towards the East]. The unquenchable desire of the Germans to possess the tremendous economic treasures of the Carpathian basin and the internationally important road leading along the valley of the Danube River, manifested itself in armed aggression and political intrigue. Under the kings of the Arpad dynasty and a succession of rulers of various other royal houses of Europe, Hungary was able to defend herself with military and diplomatic successes, and she preserved her independence and her territory remained intact.

The pressure of the Turks from the Balkans became stronger and stronger at the start of the sixteenth century and in 1526 Suleiman II, Sultan of the Turks, annihilated the Hungarian forces at Mohacs with his numerous and overpowering army. In this battle Lajos Jagiello, the last of the Hungarian kings of the so-called "mixed" royal dynasties, lost his life and he left no heirs to the throne. As a consequence of this, the Hungarian crown went to Ferdinand I of Hapsburg in compliance with a family agreement concluded in 1491 between Ulaszlo II, (Wladislav) the Hungarian king and Michael of Hapsburg, the German emperor. Following the ancient tradition to elect their kings, one part of the Hungarian nation also confirmed him to be the ruler; at the same time other parts of the nation elected Janos Zapolya, Prince of Transylvania, to be ruler and through this action expressed their mistrust of foreigners.

From this moment on Hungary was divided into three parts: the western part called "The Hungarian Kingdom," the eastern part which was the Transylvania domain, and the southern part which was occupied by the Turks. The descendants of Ferdinand I continued to rule the Hungarian Kingdom until 1918; in Transylvania the rulers were elected until 1691, at which time this territory again became part of the Hungarian Kingdom. The territories held by the Turks were returned to the Hungarian crown when the Turkish occupation forces were driven out of the country.

During the Hapsburg rule of Hungary, of almost four hundred years, one conspiracy, revolt, and fight for freedom followed another in an unbroken succession. The Hapsburgs were German emperors, Austrian archdukes, Czech and Hungarian kings, and in their immense domain they ruled in accordance to the stipulations of three different systems of constitutional law. In the German Empire they had to contend with the particular interests and requirements of the Electors and numerous smaller or greater Duchies to maintain their central might. They ruled the Austrian domain, which they considered "family possessions," in an absolutist way. They did not take the crown of Wenceslav, and it was only after the revolt of the Czechs was put down at the Battle of the White Mountain, that Bohemia became part of the Austrian crown possessions and that the absolutist system of rule was introduced there also. In Hungary, as elected rulers and crowned in observance of ancient traditions with the crown of Saint Stephen, they would have had to rule on the basis of old constitutional laws and principles which had originated in and come from Asia; instead, they more or less openly tried to introduce a centralized form of government similar to that of the Austrian Monarchy. Their reign was characterized by numerous and almost constant international strifes which rendered them unable to chase the Turks out of Hungary.

The Hungarian nation defended her independence either with eloquent words at the seldom summoned constitutional assemblies or with the sword on the battle fields during the repeated fights for independence from the omnipotent and Germanizing policies of the Hapsburgs. This represented a tremendous loss of blood for the nation and created great poverty. Large territories became depopulated and Rumanians, Bohemians, and Moravians drifted in and settled these areas. This trend was only increased in the second half of the eighteenth century during the Hapsburg rule when Schwabs, Germans from the territories of Wurtenberg, and Serbs, from the territories of the present Yugoslavia, settled these lands which had been liberated from the Turks and left without cultivation and population. Nevertheless, at the end of the eighteenth century the Hungarians, weakened in numbers and in wealth, revealed through the conspiracy of Martinovich and Sigray that their resistance against oppression was unrelenting. In 1848 the nation began a fight for freedom which made the name Lajos Kossuth known all over the world. This fight for freedom was put down by Francis Joseph I of Hapsburg but only with the aid of the 200,000 soldiers of Czar Nicholas I. After this, following the example of his predecessor Joseph II, he suspended the Hungarian Constitution and introduced an absolutist rule monitored from Vienna. During the twenty years of the "absolutist era," Hungary's economy reached the low point of poverty but her spiritual resistance survived under the influence of a flourishing literature.

Francis Joseph I, losing always more and more of his power and influence on the battle fields of Italy and Prussia, finally decided to attempt a reconciliation with the Hungarian nation.

6

In 1866, in compliance with the ancient Hungarian constitutional traditions, he had himself crowned at Budapest King of Hungary, and in 1867 the Viennese Imperial Government concluded at Budapest the "Reconciliation of 1867" with the constitutional Royal Hungarian Government. This was the start of the era of dualism. In accordance with the stipulations of the Reconciliation were formed a common Imperial and Royal Army, a common Imperial and Royal Ministry of Foreign Affairs, and common Austro-Hungarian Bank which had its seat in Vienna and which had control of the monetary system with exclusive rights in both the Hungarian and Austrian parts of the Austro-Hungarian Monarchy, and the two countries became one customs unit. This "Law of Reconciliation," from a legal standpoint, is a new Hungarian Constitution which abridges the Hungarian constitutional rights by making the Army and Foreign Affairs in common with those of Austria. The new Hungarian Constitution of 1867 was defended by the Royal Hungarian Government, backed by the majority of the "Liberal Party" of "Party of 67." This party changed its name to "Party of Labor" in 1900. Their policies were opposed by the "Party of 48" which insisted upon the elimination of the "common Army," the "common Foreign Affairs," the "Note Bank," and customs systems. This situation caused many grave parliamentary crises; the Party of 1848 demanded the restitution of the unabridged Hungarian Constitution and a change of the Austro-Hungarian Real Union into a Personal Union. It is interesting to note that thereby they recognized the right of the Hapsburg dynasty to the Hungarian throne.

In 1918, the First World War became critical for the central powers, and the revolutionary symptoms were manifested in both parts of the Austro-Hungarian Monarchy. The revolutionary element removed Charles IV, Emperor of Austria, from his exalted position and dethroned the Hapsburg family. In Hungary the so-called "Aster Revolution" did not direct its edge towards the person of the king; nevertheless, Charles IV thought it advisable to abdicate on November 16, 1918 and upon this the misled masses declared "The Hungarian Peoples Republic." For a few months the president of this republic was the Count Mihály Károlyi of cursed memory; the cowardly and misinformed Karolyi eventually turned the country over to the mercies of the Communist Bela Kun.

This brief sketch of Hungarian history brings us to the recognition of the causes of the following two historical facts: 1. That the Hungarian nation, having led for one thousand years a defensive battle against German imperialism, had developed a mistrust of and antipathy for the Germans. These feelings were by no means improved by the Austrian and German conceit and demanding attitudes, which may be observed even today, and the extensive area of the German Empire of the Hohenzollern. 2. That the currents of European history and the role of

7

the Hapsburg German-Roman Empire, later the Hapsburg Austrian Empire, created the impression in international life as though the Hungarian nation would belong to the "spheres of interest" of the Germans. The European diplomacy did not see Hungary and her real role in the German "sphere of interest;" Europe had different problems and it neglected to evaluate the matter and forgot about it. Hungary was steered towards oblivion. The Germans, those of the Empire, and also the Austrians, saw to it that Hungary was enveloped in the veil of darkness, and they advertized the Hungarian nation as an impatient, rebellious, and uncouth mass of people. This is comprehendable because the Hungarians had caused much trouble for the Germans. On the other hand, if the European powers had recognized the value of the Hungarian nation and the value of her role in the Central European region, they could have used her as a checkmate in the back of the Germans..

What did Hungary do to change this international attitude? Almost nothing. With one or two exceptions (in the times of Louis XIV, King of France, and in those of Napoleon I) in the first part of her history because she was very occupied with her domestic affairs and with her wars against the Turks, and later on (after 1867) because of her loyalty to the dynasty.

In 1914 the Hungarians became involved in the First World War, again creating the impression that they served the German's imperialistic trends and belonged in the German "sphere of interest." Today it is known fact that our Government took a stand against the declaration of war; nevertheless, with great courage and loyalty they fought the war because the Hungarian soldier is heroic and disciplined. The treaties of Versailles, St. Germain, and Trianon concluding the World War changed the basic geo-political aspects of Central Europe. The shining empire of the Hohenzollern was transformed by the Weimar Constitution into the "German Reich" with a constitution for the republic and also with diminished territories. The German speaking parts of the Austrian Empire formed the "Austrian Federated Republic." The historical Hungarian Empire became the independent Hungarian Kingdom, formed of her Hungarian speaking territories, and the Treaty of Trianon forbade the Hapsburgs to take the Hungarian Royal Throne. Czechoslovakia was formed of the Bohemian, Moravian domains of the Austrian Empire and of the territories of Hungary inhabited by Slovaks and Ruthenians. Rumania obtained the Austrian Bukovina and the Hungarian Transylvania. The Yugoslav kingdom was formed of Serbia and southern Hungarian territories, Croatia and Slavonia, the Austrian Dalmatia, Krajna, the city of Goertz, and Gradiska.

The Hungarian kingdom as shaped by the Treaty of Trianon had lost approximately sixty per cent of its territories and eighty per cent of its natural resources. The people of the mutilated Hungary, (along with the inhabitants of the territories detached from the country) at first were greatly surprised by this fact and could not comprehend it. In the first part of the twentieth century (we could regard these years as a "romantic period"), there were several attempts to change this status. As the time passed the realization grew that it was beyond Hungary's capabilities to convince the opposing moral and material forces of her just cause and to demand of them recognition of her rights. Thus, the devices of "No, no never" and "Return everything" were born. These ruled the souls of the population of mutilated Hungary and the actions of every Government between the two world wars.

After this I shall start with the narration of the details of the German-Hungarian relationship as it developed between the two world wars, mentioning that in doing so I have used many of my personal experiences and observations.

In my study entitled "Hungary and Mussolini" I presented the development of the relationship of Hungary and Italy into an intimate friendship. Immediately after the termination of the First World War, Hungary and Germany began diplomatic relations (Hungary sent an ambassador to Berlin, and Germany sent one to Budapest), but the political atmosphere between the two countries may have been labeled as only courteous.

The socialist atmosphere of Germany and her domestic crises and bloody strifes did by no means present an attractive picture to the Hungarian Governments, who were Christian, nationalist, and anti-Marxist (rightist) and who were striving to stabilize their domestic affairs. On the other hand, the Germans were not interested in the mutilated and economically valueless Hungary which was wedged between hostile nations with undefendable frontiers.

In 1925 General Hindenburg became the president of the German Republic and one could have expected that the general conditions in the Reich were going to be stabilized. Because of this expectation, the Hungarian Government sent Kálmán Kánya, an experienced professional diplomat of the Imperial and Royal Foreign Service School, as Ambassador to Berlin, with the purpose of developing the Hungarian-German political relations and of establishing economic connections by making use of his intimate and personal friendship with the general-president and other valuable connections. But the party political clashes did not cease in Germany, and on January 3, 1933, after several government crises, Hindenburg designated Adolf Hitler to be the Chancellor of the Reich. With this the "Machtubernahme" (the "Take over of the power") was consumated, and Hitler promulgated in Nuremberg the formation of the Third Reich (August 30, 1933). Simultaneously, the "Gleichschaltung" (equalization) started; that is to say that the personnel of all offices and institutions of the Government or under Government control became subject to substitution by reliable members of the German National Socialist Party.

Already at the "take over of power" and in the grave party political fights surrounding it, Kalman Kanya, not sympathizing with the formation of the totalitarian system, gradually lost his connections to the leading circles of Germany and his positions became more and more impossible in Berlin. Therefore, Gyula Gombos, Minister President, called him back and entrusted him with the portfolio of the Ministry of Foreign Affairs, thereby replacing Endre Puky, Foreign Minister. His successor in Berlin was Gyorgy Masszirevics, also an old professional and experienced diplomat. But he could not produce any results in the surroundings of the Third Reich and soon, in 1935, he was assigned to be the Ambassador to London. He was succeeded in Berlin by Dome Sztoyai (Stojakovics), a general who held the rank of a colonel in the First World War in the Imperial and Royal Army and then in 1918 he entered the services of the Yugoslav Army and was promoted to general. Later again he thought it better to seek employment in the Hungarian Army and there he was taken in, preserving his rank of general. Soon he was sent to be the Military Attaché at the Hungary Embassy in Berlin.

Dome Sztoyai was a very bad looking man, did not speak Hungarian very well, and had certain other limitations. But in Berlin he gained the trust of Ribbentropp and Goering, and several other "greats" and became a loyal interpreter of the interests of the Third Reich in Budapest. Thus it is quite clear that Hungary's foreign political representation which was inadequate during the period immediately preceding and following the "Machtubernahme," could have resulted in rather disagreeable consequences in political and especially in economical matters.

In my study "Hungary and Mussolini," I described how very much Hungary was concerned with Austria's attitude in the matter of the "Anschluss," and how much effort was put forth to hinder such a move. It could have been assumed that the Third Reich was going to precipitate the annexation of the Austro-German territories; on the other hand, the "easing up" policies of the Third Reich in respect to the obligations stated in the Treaty of Versailles stood in the center of the interests of the Hungarian Government who was trying to obtain a modification of the Treaty of Trianon. Also the increasing Hungarian production could not do without the tremendous potentiality of the German market. Gyula Gombos and Kalman Kanya here also followed the customary diplomatic practice of sending a very able emissary to clarify the entangled and unclear situation. Taking into consideration the personal visit of Gyula Gombos to Berlin, their choice fell on Vitez Andras Mecser.

Who was this gentleman? Andras Mecser came from a civil servant family and was a professional officer. He served in the rank of captain during the First World War in the "No. 13 Jasz-Kun," Hussar regiment. He was a mediocre officer and a mediocre horseman, but with slyness and outstanding tenacity he carried out several successful armed actions and earned exceptionally high decorations for them. In 1916 he was taken prisoner by the Russians but escaped from Siberia disguised as a Russian Jew and soon reported back to duty at his regiment. In 1917 he was detailed as the Military Attaché of the then Imperial and Royal Embassy in Berlin, where with his wit and likeable character he acquired many friends in large circles of Germany.

During this time, he became an intimate friend of a German officer called Darre. This Darre became Minister of Agriculture in Adolf Hitler's Government in 1933. Mecser, after the fall of the Dual Monarchy and the disbanding of the Army, reported to duty at the counter revolutionary nationalist government formed at Szeged and participated in the reorganization of the national army. Here, he made the acquaintance of Gyula Gombos and other important personalities who later played roles in the life of the nation. In 1920 he left the military service, married and became an agronomist managing his wife's beautiful estate, breeding horses, and developing special hybrid seeds. He was especially successful in developing the corn seed known as "Gold Rain" [in German "Goldregen"] which with the help of Darre was sold later on in Germany with great success. On one of his numerous business trips, Mecser was in Munich when Hitler gave a speech at one of the mass meetings of the Party. Mecser participated at the meeting, and while under the influence of the speech, he offered the profits of his business transaction to the purpose of the National Socialist movement. Upon this he was introduced to the Fuehrer. The friendship of Darre and this monetary contribution laid the foundations for Mecser's position in Germany.

In evaluating and classifying the personality of Andras Mecser, we want to emphasize only his various travels to Germany and his connections to German leading circles which enabled him to solve the problems arising out of the realization of the aims and purposes entrusted to him in their full extent.

Hitler, avoiding the official way, invited Gyula Gombos to a private meeting. This visit took place under absolute secret circumstances on June 16, 1933. Gombos flew from Budapest to Berlin and there, at the airport, was received by a gentleman who took him to Hitler. The two men talked for more than two hours alone after which Gombos immediately flew back to Budapest. The press was not notified previously of this visit, and later all that was said was that such a meeting had transpired, that the talks had been conducted in a friendly atmosphere, and that their aim was only to establish a general orientation. There is no doubt that Kalman Kanya, Minister of Foreign Affairs, knew of this visit and obtained detailed information as to the happenings, but Gombos himself never made any statements about them, not even in his most intimate circle of friends.

One time while talking to me about something entirely different, he made the following hint: "We are looking towards very difficult times."

The well-oriented people assumed that at this meeting Gombos could not talk too much. Instead he listened and Hitler must have told him everything about his future plans, notably the division of Czechoslovakia, and the fact that he would probably not object if Hungary regained Upper Hungary, although he would not permit the Rumanian and Yugoslav territories to be touched. To this day there is tangible evidence that the conversation took such turns. There is one fact, however, to be considered that after this meeting the Hungarian German commercial relations began to increase noticeably.

The Berlin visit of Gombos caused great surprise in Hungary and was received with very mixed feelings. Some were rather critical upon receiving the news because they considered the step taken by Gombos as superfluous, too early, and rather risky because of the attitude of the Great and Little Ententes. Others were fearful that this step might bring a change in the Italian orientation of Hungarian policy held by previous Hungarian Governments and even by Gyula Gombos himself, and therefore, considered this step unwarranted and without good reason. There were, however, also those who, knowing very well certain reserved attitudes of Gyula Gombos towards the Austrian and German Reich, had confidence in his reasoning and persuasive speech. These were of the opinion that he aimed to obtain first hand information from the German Chancellor who had come into power by noteworthy methods. They were sure Hitler had wanted to clear up some questions and to gain his cooperation in the solution of the questions of the Danube Line and the Carpathian Basin.

Abroad the Berlin visit of Gombos caused great surprise and unfavorable reaction among all except Italy. It may be assumed, however, that Mussolini had been previously informed and approved of this step. Some later occurrences also indicate that another great power, namely France, was influenced by this event and drew certain conclusions from it which resulted in beneficial moves towards Hungary; for instance, the reorganization of her Army.

On July 20, 1933, only about six weeks after the secret visit of Gombos, Engelbert Dollfuss, the Austrian Chancellor, a great antagonist of the Anschluss and a trustworthy friend of the Hungarian, Italian, and Austrian alliance, was gunned down by some persons who were quite probably close to the German National Socialist Party. Gyula Gombos may have known about preparations for such an attempt because he mentioned to the writer of these lines, "They may eliminate one of these days this poor Dollfuss," and it is sure that he notified the Chancellor about the great peril threatening his life.

In Hungary this bloody event caused great consternation

because it was considered a sign that the Third Reich was going to end Austria's independence quite soon. It was also known in Hungary that the successor of Dollfuss, Kurt Schuschnigg, was sympathetic to the German intentions; the nomination of Franz Papen as the German Ambassador to Vienna was also considered a sign of the over increasing pressure by the Reich.

The first signs of the "difficult times" manifested themselves. In my study entitled "Hungary and Mussolini" I gave an ample description of those diplomatic moves which led to the solidification of the Hungarian and Italian friendly connections in the times following the above happenings and which aimed, by all means, to hinder the "Anschluss" (in spite of the continued intrigues of Benes). During these years Gombos paid a visit to Ankara and Warsaw with the aim to create with the help of Turkey and Poland a line of defense against the imperialistic threatening from the West and from the East. These negotiations proved to be futile. The Turks concluded treaties with the Russians; and the Poles, on the other hand, with the French.

In September 1935, Gombos, this time accompanied by Kanya, paid another visit to Berlin. This visit did not have a prearranged agenda, and the Hungarian public was told soon after that Hitler had given a full account of his future intentions and had again emphasized that he was willing to support Hungarian claims against Czechoslovakia but that he would not permit Rumania and Yugoslavia to be touched. It is possible that during the first visit, in support of his domestic political aims, Gombos concluded a pact with Goring. The existence of such a pact was probably revealed to Kalman Daranyi, the successor of Gombos after his death, but if so he kept it a secret also. Those who somehow were able to obtain information about it were of the opinion that Gombos concluded this pact to counteract National Socialist and Pan-Germanic agitations which at that time had already started to be very noticeable. In 1936 Miklos Horthy, the regent of Hungary, paid a visit to Hitler in Berchtesgaden. The purpose of this visit was deer hunting and it is probable that political questions were discussed. In the circle of his friends the Regent repeatedly recounted that he, Horthy, emphasized the purposefulness of an English alliance to Hitler.

In the meantime, on March 7, 1936, the Third Reich occupied the Rhine territory. This outstanding event, which was accepted without any action by the Entente powers, basically changed the foreign political trends of the powers located east of the Rhine River. Yugoslavia, a member of the Little Entente and friendly to the English-French Alliance hurried to declare that she would never think of attacking the Third Reich and that she sympathized with her. Yugoslavia's example was followed by Rumania, another member of the Little Entente who was especially liked and pampered by the French. The third member of the Little Entente, Czechoslovakia, confident of her treaty concluded with the USSR in 1935, increased the intrigues in Vienna to entice Austria into the sphere of interest of the Little Entente. Mussolini, who at that time was strongly discouraged by the attitude of the Geneva League of Nations towards the Italian-Abyssinian conflict, reduced the pace of his diplomatic advancement towards France.

In Hungary these events created great consternation, especially since under the influence of National Socialist principle in Hungary political opposition groups had developed and a strong pan-Germanic movement had started among the German speaking inhabitants of the country. Hungary tried a rapprochment to Yugoslavia (the writer of these lines upon request of Gombos also negotiated personally with the Yugoslav Royal Ambassador at Budapest about the development of friendly relations in the field of sports and allied youth activities, but got a courteous refusal).

On October 6, 1936, Gyula Gombos died in a hospital in Munich succumbing to a kidney disease of many years. On October 10, 1936, the Regent appointed Kalman Daranyi to be Minister President and immediately following this action strange and disturbing symptoms appeared.

In the internal political life, numerous opposition groups emerged, shouting National Socialist slogans, and the Hungarian Schwabs (ethnic Germans) with the support of the newspapers of the German Reich, started in our country as well as abroad, actions against and attacks on the new Government. It soon became obvious to the foreign political field that Daranyi was not welcomed by Berlin, and there were several statements made from that source in connection with Rumania, Yugoslavia, and even that of Czechoslovakia, affecting the sensitivity of Hungary. The Hungarian Government also became cognizant of a letter written by Mussolini to Hitler, first mentioning an Italian-German Axis.

There was another source which spread the news that instead of a Budapest-Rome-Vienna block there was a Budapest-Prague-Vienna block in creation. This of course was started in Prague with the purpose of increasing the tension between Berlin and Budapest.

In Hungary Daranyi began appeasing and equalizing in an attempt to halt the movements of the opposition which were sporadically supported by the youth and the circles of the intelligentsia. Therefore, he contacted the writer of these lines (who since 1932 had been the president of the "Federation of Social Association" [abbreviated T.E.S.Z.] composed of about six thousand national organizations, and entrusted me with the task of increasing the activities of the Federation which involved activity of a non-political nature, propagating unity and zeal and loyalty and to invite the valuable elements of the turbulent youth into this outstanding patriotic work.

14

In diplomatic matters Daranyi carried on the attempts of the previous Hungarian Governments for a rapprochement to Yugoslavia who not only responded to the friendly policies of the Third Reich but seemed to be agreeable to rapprochement after Ciano's visit to Belgrade [Translator's remark: Count Galeazzo Ciano, Minister of Foreign Affairs of Italy] which represented new trends of Italian foreign political intentions (see my study entitled "Hungary and Mussolini"). In spite of the friendly gestures by Berlin to Rumania, Budapest remained facilitated by the attitudes of Bucharest. The former friendly relationship with Italy was continued. The Hungarian politics in respect to the Third Reich became very, very difficult because of the touchy problem of the Austrian question and the disagreeable attitudes of the Hitler regime manifesting themselves everywhere, and mainly perhaps because of the mistrust and antipathy for the Germans which increased day by day in Hungary.

This may be illustrated with an example characterizing this particular situation. The Federation of Social Associations created committees to increase relationships with friendly nations (we had Hungarian-Italian, Hungarian-Turkish, Hungarian-Polish, et cetera, committees). Kalman Daranyi, upon the demand of the German Ambassador at Budapest, told the writer of these lines to form a Hungarian-German committee. I was unable to provide members and a president for such a committee because my request received negative replies from all sides. This very painful predicament was ended by Daranyi who finally nominated a Hungarian-German committee, consisting of forty members, and designated as its president his good friend Andras Tasnadi-Nagy, former Minister of Justice, who spoke very poor German.

The Hossbach Conference took place on November 5, 1937, and it became obvious that Hitler wanted to annex Austria and also the Moravian and Bohemian parts of Czechoslovakia. On November 20, 1937, Kalman Daranyi and Kalman Kanya, accompanied by a few experts, traveled to Berlin. The negotiations focused on economic questions and later the Hungarian public learned that the Germans had made rather insistent demands in respect to agricultural products. The Conference also dealt with the status of the Hungarian ethnic Germans (Schwabs). This question was, however, settled in a "satisfactory" way by Balint Homan, Minister of Education, who was also present. It was only on November 25 that political questions came to debate and even then for only about two hours, and it is quite possible that Hitler at that time informed the Hungarians of his plans for the future, namely, the division of Czechoslovakia. Kanya later made the following remark at a party in the presence of the writer of these lines: "Hitler is not a fool to seek something beyond the Carpathians." The foreign political atmosphere appeared to be less tense and I remember well one of Kalman Daranyi's New Year's radio speeches in which he stated: "The Hungarian Government wishes to convince the foreign powers of her rightful claims in a peaceful way."

The Berlin negotiations and Daranyi's radio address had two way consequences in the Parliamentary and press circles. Some really believed that the political atmosphere was easing and imagined that it was inopportune to implement the plans of the Third Reich and that the "Anschluss" could also be dropped. This belief seemed to be supported by the idea of a Prague-Vienna-Budapest block which had been proclaimed rather boisterously by Benes; others were, however, of a contrary opinion. They were convinced that the "Anschluss" was going to be realized in the shortest possible time that the annihilation of Czechoslovakia was inevitable, and that one had to expect very grave international crises. The more informed parliamentary circles knew that the government really stood on the latter conviction and military circles urgently advised the Regent to develop the Hungarian Army. It was also known that the famous General Soos submitted to the Regent and Daranyi a memorandum in which he gave details concerning the development of the Army and certain inner political moves.

Daranyi also prepared for any critical happenings. He removed his Finance Minister Tihamer Fabinyi, who would not have been able to provide the Army with the necessary financial funds, and replaced him with Lajos Remenyi-Schneller, the outstanding financial expert. He invited Bela Imredy, the very influential president of the Hungarian National Bank, to fill the position of general economic minister. In March 1938, in an address held in the city of Gyor, he declared that he was going to appropriate one billion Pengo for development of the Army, industry and agriculture, and the funds would be provided by a special tax to be introduced. This so-called "Program of Gyor" was received with great enthusiasm everywhere in the country; the "first Jewish law," promulgated a few weeks later, seemed to ease the worried tension, but great concern was expressed about the provocative activities of the Berlin "Volks Deutsche Mittelstelle" [translated: ethnic German Central Agency].

On March 11, 1938, the "Anschluss" took place. When the writer of these lines read about the fatal turn of events, he hurried to visit Daranyi at his office. The Minister President excitedly paced up and down his room and started immediately to explain the situation. He was extremely pessimistic and he asked me to communicate his opinions to my colleagues in the Lower House of Parliament. A few days later a rumor had spread throughout the country that the German Army, occupying the Austrian territories, had stopped at the historical Austro-Hungarian frontier to give the Hungarian Army an opportunity to occupy to so-called "burgenland" and that only after they realized that the Hungarian Army units were not moving from their stations, did they continue their progress to the Trianon-Hungarian border. The authenticity of this fact is questionable but some statements coming from pertinent official sources made at later occasions make it entirely plausible. According to these statements the Hungarian Government possibly felt the occupation of the Burgenland was a risky venture considering the dubious attitudes of Paris and London.

On May 13, 1938, the Regent absolved Kalman Daranyi of his post and designated Bela Imredy to be Minister President. Daranyi really tumbled down from the peak of his popularity. The Government Party, which wanted to honor and celebrate him because of his political successes, had requested the writer of these lines to discuss with him a date for a festive luncheon. I went and visited him in his office and giving him the reason for my visit; he answered with a resigned half smile: "I think the time at the present moment is rather inopportune for such a thing because the Regent absolved me of my duties just this morning." I asked him in great consternation about the reasons of this unexpected decision and also about his successor, upon which he answered: "Do not ask the reasons, my successor is Bela Imredy." I retorted: "The party is going to topple him at his introductory speech." He answered: "I ask you very strongly, talk with your friends and persuade them to refrain from such action; they should not make the situation even more difficult." I acted in compliance to his request and the introductory address of Imredy was received with icy composure at the general assembly of the party.

Imredy was not popular in political circles nor among the general public. Everybody knew his conservative, liberal-mercantilist philosophy and were afraid that these tendencies of his would affect the advancing economic and social needs of the country; it was also common knowledge that he did not have the sympathy of Rome and of Berlin. It remains a secret what the reasons for the unexpected and apparently unwarranted decision of the Regent were and well-informed circles believed that behind all this were exclusive machinations by Imredy to gain power. Public opinion was soothed rather satisfactorily by the fact that Imredy succeeded in getting for his cabinet Count Pal Teleki, who was of great influence and esteem, and the right wing Sandor Sztranyavszky. The first of these two men, was rumored to be an Anglophile, the latter Germanophile. Kalman Kanya, the "Old Tiger," stayed on in the position of Minister of Foreign Affairs.

Four happenings are noteworthy in the foreign political sphere after the first few months of Imredy's entrance into office. Point One: Placing greater emphasis on the development of the days' commercial connections with England, Imredy appointed a commercial attaché to the Hungarian Embassy in London. Point Two: The Poles communicated with the Hungarian Government that in the event of the division of Czechoslovakia they were going to insist upon rectification of their frontier by Prague. Point Three: Yugoslavia eased her unyielding attitude towards the Hungarian minorities living in the country and expressed neutrality in the event of a German-Czechoslovakian conflict. Point Four: In the month of July, Imredy, Kanya, and the latter's deputy Count Istvan Csaky paid a courtesy visit to Rome. According to the news surrounding the event, Mussolini advised the Hungarian Minister President to introduce "social and economic reforms."

Of greater importance than any of the events enumerated above was the launching and baptism of a ship at Kiel. In Hungary, this event is regarded as the most important political move of the time. During the Minister Presidency of Kalman Daranyi, Hitler invited Regent Horthy to the festivities accompanying the launching of a German battleship. The choice for the name to be given to the ship was between "Thegetoff" and "Prinz Eugen." The name "Thegetoff" was dropped because of the Italians (Thegetoff, Austrian Admiral, beat the Italian fleet in 1866 at Lissa), and the name "Prinz Eugen" was kept. Horthy was reluctant to participate in the event since the Prinz Eugen of Savoy, Austrian General of French origin, had participated actively at the start of the Eighteenth century in the overthrow of the fight for liberty in Hungary under the Transylvanian Prince Ferenc Rakoczi II. To decide if the refusal would be an affront was a serious matter, and the political importance of the ship's christening had to be weighed carefully. The latter consideration decided the question, and in the last part of July, after great preparations, Regent Horthy, his wife, Bela Imredy and his wife, Kanya, Minister of Foreign Affairs, and General Racz, Chief of Staff, accompanied by experts, traveled to Kiel where they were received by Hitler, Ribbentropp, and Admiral Raeder and other dignitaries.

The role of the Godmother of the battleship was filled by the wife of Miklos Horthy. After the festive occasion there was a great fleet parade which was in turn followed by a gala performance at the opera house.

In following days political negotiations were conducted between Horthy and Hitler and between Kanya and Ribbentropp respectively, which dealt with the participation of Hungary in an armed action of Germany to be introduced against Czechoslovakia. These were rigidly refused by the Hungarians due to the inadequate armor, equipment, and drill of their Army. The official communiques issued pertaining to the "Kiel days" were rather unclear and contradictory, but the news spread in the Hungarian political circles that Horthy had reminded Hitler that in the event of a war the British fleet with its tremendous striking power would threaten him; on the other hand, Kanya in talking about Hungary's standpoint and interests, sometimes used pointed and aggressive tones with Ribbentropp.

Neither met by any means with the pleasure of these German "gentlemen."

During the "Kiel days" the foreign ministers of the Little Entente invited Gyorgy Bakacs-Bessenyei, our Ambassador to Belgrade, to a conference held at the Yugoslav seaside resort, Bled. These negotiations led to the agreement in which the states of the Little Entente acknowledged Hungary's right to rearm; on the other hand, Hungary renounced all acts of aggression against them, and the text of the agreement stated that other questions of mutual well-being and relations between neighbors were not yet subject to negotiation.

During this time rumors swept the country that London had written Hungary down as one who is inevitably thrown into the arms of the Third Reich; on the other hand, there were also those who pretended to know that the English public opinion was sympathetic toward the Hungarian territorial claims against the Czechs and would accept it if the Slovaks, if they so wished, returned to Hungary, the mother country. Hitler delivered a great address in Nuremberg from which some concluded that the Fuehrer was ready to arrange an agreement with Benes on the Sudeten question if the latter would grant him certain concessions which would result, of course, in the complete disregard of Hungarian territorial claims. On the other hand, we all concluded that the British Prime Minister Chamberlain, on his visit to Berchtesgaden, was going to persuade Hitler to regulate the Sudeten, Hungarian-Polish, and Carpatho-Russian questions through peaceful agreements. Somehow certain circles in Hungary knew of a letter sent by Stojadinovic, Yugoslav Prime Minister, to Count Ciano, in which he stated that in connection with the Czechoslovakian affair he would not interfere aggressively against Hungary. Also known were the contents of letters of Mussolini sent to Lord Runciman in which the Duce proposed a popular vote not only in the Sudeten dispute but also in the Hungarian question. According to rumors similar opinions were voiced by Beck, Polish Minister of Foreign Affairs, concerning the solution of the question of the Hungarian minorities in Czechoslovakia.

All this unclear and contradictory information reaching the country made the impression in Hungary that our foreign policy reached a cul de sac and that the Imredy government had committed a grave mistake with its indecision. The Hungarian press enveloped itself in great silence. Upon the basis of all this, the Hungarian Government Party (MEP) at its annual convention held in September, issued an address to the Hungarian minorities living in Czechoslovakia in the name of all Hungarians, saying that they should take the settlement of their fate in their own hands; a patriotic association the "Revisionist League" sent wires to all governments of the great powers requesting that they grant to the Hungarian minorities the right to decide about their own fate through popular vote. At the same time parliamentary circles learned that Foreign Minister Kanya had communicated to the ambassadors of our country in Berlin, London, and Paris, and that he personally had communicated the same to Knox, British Ambassador to Budapest, that Hungary was going to request in a note from Czechoslovakia to allow the fate of those territories in which Hungarians lived in majority to be decided by popular vote and that he had the cooperation of Poland in this matter also. Very little was heard by Parliamentary and press circles from Paris and London about this action (if there were any they must have been very indecisive.) It was learned, however, that Bucharest was spreading the rumor in the capitals of the great powers that Hungary wanted to annex the entire Slovakia.

During this time an invitation from Hitler to Imredy and Kanya to come to Berchtesgaden was received; and Ciano increasingly urged Hungary and Poland to augment their pressure in the question of the Czechoslovakian minorities. Imredy and Kanya traveled to Berchtesgaden, but meager notices were issued as to the happenings at the negotiations. I was told by an acquaintance who was in the Ministry of Foreign Affairs (either Count Istvan Csaky or Alfred Nicki) that Hitler had made up his mind to settle the Czechoslovakian question within three weeks and if necessary even by force of arms; and that if Hungary were going to be passive she was going to play away her chances. I also heard later, from a similar source, that Hitler communicated his decision to the Polish Government and to Mussolini. As a result of the above visit, the Hungarian press dealt at large with all questions of Hungarian minorities and their right to a popular vote decision. The "Revisionist League" and the semi-official "Association of Foreign Affairs" organized mass demonstrations. Some army units were called to arms. Poland ordered army mobilization along the Czechoslovakian border, and there were boisterous mass demonstrations in Warsaw and in other Polish cities.

The Hungarian public opinion was very disappointed to learn that London objected to the Hungarian attitude and opposed the Hungarian "mobilization" and that the Poles obtained similar admonitions from the same source. The Hungarian public opinion also was informed of the fact that Prague declined all sorts of territorial concessions.

At the same time the world famous Hitler-Chamberlain meeting at Godesberg took place and it became known that the English Prime Minister was unpleasantly surprised and was rather excited about Hitler's communiques pertaining to the claims of Hungary and Poland. It also became known in Hungary that the British wanted to deal only with the Sudeten question and that they wanted to postpone all other solutions to a later date. It also became known that Benes had instigated Soviet Russia to interfere with armed forces, and that Russia called the Hungarian claims "follies."

What was done in Hungary? Some advised caution, others advised force; the Government did not cease to repeatedly invite German attention to Hungary's claims against Czechoslovakia and emphasized towards Yugoslavia (from where there were no dangerous moves to be expected) and towards Rumania her peaceful intentions. On September 29, 1938, the "Munich Conference" was opened at which the English, French, German, and Italian Governments participated through their representatives and Hungary and Poland sent observers (Count Istvan Csaky, Deputy Foreign Minister who carried a personal letter of Regent Horthy to Hitler and Major General Vitez Laszlo Szabo, who was our military attaché at Rome and an intimate friend of Mussolini). I already stated the details pertaining to the Hungarian question that was at this conference in my study entitled "Hungary and Mussolini." Hitler brought up the Hungarian claims only after having been reminded of them by Mussolini, trying to manifest through this his mistrust and anger towards the Hungarians. The decision of the Conference read in one of the annexes as follows: "The modalities pertaining to the solutions of the Sudeten question are going to be applicable in accordance with usual diplomatic procedures to the Hungarian and Polish questions also." This decision by no means satisfied the Hungarian expectations and created new entanglements. It left open the Slovak and Ruthenian questions.

I will attempt to give the details of the situations created which by force led to the so-called "First Viennese Arbitrage." In compliance with the decisions made at Munich by the "Great Powers" [Great Britain, France, China, Italy, USA, Germany, later Russia; here the writer meant England and Germany], the Hungarian Government offered to negotiate with Prague about her territorial claims. The Czechs, however, wanted to postpone the entire affair. We became aware, however, that although the Slovaks were insisting on independence, some circles in their country would have liked to return to Hungary instead. The Slovaks decided at their mass meeting at Zsolna [in Czech, Zlin] to detach themselves from Czechoslovakia and to form an independent Slovak Republic. The Ruthenians formed two groups: the Carpatho-Ruthenians who would have liked very much to join Hungary, and the Ukrainian Slovaks who turned for spiritual leadership towards the Russians. Only a few days after the Munich Conference Poland moved into the territories which she claimed and declared her desire to have a common frontier with Hungary; this would have meant, of course, that the Ruthenian territories would be turned over to Hungary. The Rumanians objected to all territorial concessions made to Hungary, and stated that they were going to hinder the annexation of the Slovak and Ruthenian territories by Hungary, even if it meant resorting to arms. Although the Yugoslavs acknowledged the rights of Hungary to the territories where Hungarians were in the majority, they did not approve of the annexation of the territories inhabited by Slovaks and Ruthenians.

From the English we were informed that London desired a peaceful solution of the Czecho-Slovakian territorial questions. No information reached us from the French and the Italians who at first seemed to think well of the orientation of the Slovaks and Ruthenians towards Hungary and later, maybe in view of the Yugoslav objections, pressed for a solution of only the territorial questions which pertained to the Hungarian minority. Hitler immediately declared that he would recognize a Slovak Republic, if formed, averting through this an eventual adherence of the new state to Hungary, and he emphatically advised the Hungarian Government to conduct negotiations pertaining to territorial claims as soon as possible with the new Slovak Government. In regard to the question of a common Hungarian-Polish frontier he expressed mistrust and refused to consider it because he saw in such a move a Polish-Hungarian intrigue directed against his interests.

It was under such circumstances that the negotiations were begun by the Hungarian and Slovak Governments in 1933 on a ship anchored at the city of Komarom. The Hungarian Government was represented by Count Teleki and Kanya, and the Slovaks were represented by Minister President Tiso heading the delegation (in which also appeared a Ruthenian political representative.) The negotiations started in a very uneasy atmosphere because Bela Imredy, Prime Minister, had ordered his representatives not to ask but to "demand." Kanya, on the other hand, wanted to negotiate in the French language which was not spoken by any of the Slovak representatives. Thus, the negotiations ended quite soon without the least results. The Hungarian Government had again turned up a dead-end street.

This situation caused great surprise and ire in Hungarian Parliamentary circles because they did not trust the foreign political weight of the Imredy Government, because they feared that we would fall out of Hitler's favor completely, that as a consequence of that Mussolini would withdraw, and the sympathetic attitude of the Poles would change also. My colleagues in Parliament selected me to visit Kalman Daranyi, who had acquired at previous visits certain prestige before Hitler, in order to persuade him to travel to the "Fuehrer" and make an attempt to save what could still be saved. Upon my request Daranyi immediately received me at his residence (as far as I know after me he had a visit from Deputies Janos Szeder and Istvan Milotay). He categorically refused to accept the idea of an eventual visit to Berlin, however, saying that he did not want to interfere with Imredy's political actions. Only after I reminded him that personal controversies should not influence a step to be taken in the interest of the country,

22

did he reverse his decision; and after having cleared his visit with the Regent and Imredy, he flew to Berlin.

When he returned after a few days he called me and told me the details of his visit. Hitler had received him immediately, and as he paced up and down in the room he had told him in very bitter words about the "mistrusting, uncomprehending, two-faced attitude of the Hungarians," and then stopping in front of Daranyi he had asked him: "Why do the Hungarians not love me?" Daranyi very quietly had answered: "Because why, for instance, do you want to give the city of Pozsony [in German: Pressburg; and in Czech: Bratislava] to the Slovaks?" Upon which Hitler had retorted: "They asked me to do this in a memorandum signed by seventy thousand persons." Daranyi had answered: "Do you want to see a memorandum signed by one hundred thousand in which they ask to be attached to Hungary?" Hitler made an angry gesture and then began to smile and asked: "Well, what do you really want?" and then they began to negotiate in earnest and these negotiations promised to clarify the situation. The situation, however, did not clarify itself; on the contrary, it steadily became more and more aggravated.

The Ruthenians requested a popular election, and thus the Czechs sent military reinforcements to Carpatho-Ruthenia and placed the city of Ungvar under martial law. The Poles pressed for a decision in the Hungarian-Polish question; and Hungarian volunteer fighter units ("Guards in rags") drifted into Ruthenian territories and this resulted in skirmishes and great losses on both sides. The Slovaks made proposals to the Hungarian Government but Budapest did not consider them fit for negotiation. Imredy thought to mobilize the Army, in part, but would have liked it if the Munich "Four Power" conference would decide all contested questions. He sent Count Istvan Csaky to Rome to negotiate for a stand to be taken by Mussolini. The Duce was relieved by Hungarian plans to mobilize and by the consideration of the question by the Four Powers. Ciano contacted Ribbentropp by telephone about this matter. However, Ribbentropp was against any decision by the Four Powers because he was assured that London and Paris would take a stand in favor of Prague. This assumption was not quite correct because we learned later that London had been in favor of our solution of self-determination, and that Paris had been sympathetic to a Hungarian-Polish frontier but that both powers were hesitant to participate in a new Four Power conference. The Polish Minister of Foreign Affairs Beck paid a visit to the King of Rumania but found a rigid withdrawal by the King. Mussolini was then inclined to accept a role in a dual court arbitrage and Ciano made a proposal to Ribbentropp to that effect. But the latter declined this proposition also. In the meantime, the Czechs were becoming more and more aggresive in Carpatho-Ruthenia and the Rumanians threatened to mobilize completely. In this rather tense atmosphere the Hungarian Government turned to Berlin and Rome and asked them to solve the contested questions with a two-power decision.

On October 30, Ciano and Ribbentropp arrived in Vienna, and there they rendered the first Viennese Arbitrage decision. The Hungarian Government was represented by Count Pal Teleki and Count Istvan Csaky. At the negotiations an unfavorable impression was created by Ribbentropp's complete silence. It was Ciano who laughingly drew lines of the new Hungarian-Slovakian frontier into the maps prepared for the purpose. Of the great northern cities, the new frontier left the old Hungarian crowning city of Pozsony [Translator's note: today the Czech Bratislava] to the Czechs but gave to Hungary the center of Hungarian culture, Kassa [at present the Czech Kosice], where lie the ashes of the great Ferenc Rakoczi II. Also returned to the mother country were the cities of Leva, Losonc, Ungvar, and Munkacs; the two latter ones were returned without settling the Ruthenian or Polish-Hungarian border question. Ciano later told the wife of Secretary of State Baron Gyorgy Pronay that he traced the new Hungarian border really only out of gratitude to the Hungarians.

In the meantime, the Hungarians waited tensely to hear the reactions of the English and the French. Soon we were informed that the English Government communicated to our Ambassador to London Barcza that they accepted the news of the Arbitrage with pleasure and contentment. The French official circles did not emit any particular statements, but the French papers emphasized that the Arbitrage decisions eliminated some very grave entanglements. This news only increased the happiness of the Hungarian nation about the return of the Hungarian inhabited territories of the Upper Hungary. More disagreeable, however, was the news which struck the Hungarian public a few days later that the Third Reich had annexed on Slovak territory the cities of Deveny and the village of Pozsony-Ligetfalu, both of which were of mixed Hungarian-German population.

The Hungarian military and civilian Government hurried to occupy those territories which had been returned through the decisions, but the question of the northern Ruthenian territory and the cities of Ungvar and Munkacs was still open. The Hungarian public and the Polish Government urged that a solution be reached. It was only in the middle of November that the Hungarian Government, in view of the the unrest felt among the Ruthenians, decided to take the necessary steps. It was indispensable to obtain the approval of Berlin and Rome. Berlin categorically opposed everything. Rome, however, was in favor of decisive action and even promised to contribute airplanes and air support to an armed settlement of the question. The Italians retracted their promise once they were informed of the standpoint of Berlin, and declared that they had to adhere to the decision of the former.

Pretty soon a German-Italian mutual diplomatic note was sent to Budapest which demanded that Hungary adhere strictly to the decisions of Vienna and warned her not to count on any help in any aggressive action; she alone would be responsible and the sole initiator in case of doing so.

While the foreign political happenings were rather turbulent, the internal politics — largely under their influence — also became the scene of outstanding events. Political circles seemed to observe a cardinal change in the attitude of Minister President Bela Imredy following the first Viennese Arbitrage decision. He, who was considered as a liberal mercantilist leaning heavily toward the opinions of the Entente powers, seemed to bow before the greatness and power of the Third Reich. He exchanged some members of his Cabinet for such personalities who were in sympathy with the politics of Hitler, and thus he replaced the outstanding Minister of Foreign Affairs Kalman Kanya, who never was in the favor of Berlin, with Count Istvan Csaky. He also submitted the draft of a very strong Jewish law to the Houses of Parliament; and in one of the ministerial councils, proposals of a rather totalitarian nature were being made for a change of the Constitution. [Note: these were never acted upon].

These last facts came to the attention of the writer of these lines in the following manner. Late one evening, I was with a few friends of mine (I remember representatives Ferenc Krudy, Janos Szeder, Kalman Shvoy) in the party club of the Government Party and we were discussing the situation in one of the parlors, when suddenly the General Secretary of the Party, Bela Marton, rushed into the room and enthusiastically shouted while waving a bundle of papers in hand: "Gentlemen, Bela decided a change to the Constitution, the text of which is here in my hand." He was a well-known sympathizer of the Germans and of German origin. We received this news with great consternation and after a few minutes of astounded silence we fired away with many questions at Marton who became suddenly rather secretive and finally departed. We immediately decided that we were going to do everything to make the plan impossible. To my knowledge it never came to discussion at all.

Very shortly after this, Vitez Gyorgy Bobory, one of the vice-presidents of the Lower House and a very good friend of mine, invited me to visit him in his Parliamentary chambers. I immediately went to see him and he received me with the following words: "Gabor, I have to tell you very disagreeable news. According to some documents given to me by Count Antal Sigray, a representative of the opposition party, Bela Imredy is of Jewish descent, and he asked me to publish those. What shall I do?" Bobory was a very honest and noble minded gentleman through and through. It was not very difficult to persuade him that in such a case it was best to do nothing.

Sigray and his colleague, Representative Karoly Rassay [Rasch means German version of the name], however, also sent the documents to the Regent who in a very dramatic conversation asked Imredy to reveal the truth of this matter. Imredy could not make a definite denial and he submitted his abdication and gave the reasons for it in a speech delivered to the House of Representatives.

In connection with these domestic political events, I must mention a very important diplomatic step taken prior to the fall of Bela Imredy. Count Istvan Csaky, in his capacity as the new Minister of Foreign Affairs, traveled to Berlin and there signed the Italian-German-Japanese "Anti-Comintern Pact." The Imredy Government had decided to take this important step and to create thus a favorable atmosphere for a decision to be made in the Ruthenian question and for its final settlement in Berlin.

On February 16, 1939, the Regent designated Count Pal Teleki to be Imredy's successor in the chair of the Hungarian Minister President. This decision was received with great pleasure and satisfaction everywhere in the country because his personality, his great knowledge and experience, and very valuable foreign connections and patriotism had earned him public respect, trust, and popularity. The English and French press received his nomination with great sympathy, whereas the German press manifested its usual mistrust, assumptions, and disagreeable attitude. Teleki removed some rather extremist members of the Cabinet but kept Count Istvan Csaky in the chair of Minister of Foreign Affairs even though some people considered him a great sympathizer of the Germans.

These charges were without foundation. The writer of these lines knew the Minister of Foreign Affairs and his entire family. They were an ancient Transylvanian and Upper Hugarian (of the county of Szepes) clan which had given to the country over the centuries many outstanding personalities such as clergymen, soldiers, and administrators. Istvan Csaky was not a friend of the Germans but a Hungarian patriot who in a given situation sought German and Italian support only for the benefits it would bring to the solution and satisfaction of the Hungarian national problems, and this was the game of cards he played. He agreed quite definitely heart and soul with Teleki's idea to form a north-south block, that is to say, a Polish, Hungarian, Yugoslav, Bulgarian, and Turkish defensive unit. Consequently, he was also a follower of the foreign political concepts of Gyula Gombos.

On February 15 the Third Reich moved into Bohemia and Moravia. These events preceded Teleki's entrance into the office of Minister President, made it possible for Teleki, once in the office, to follow up immediately on the solution of the Ruthenian question, especially since Berlin and Rome had communicated to him through their Berlin Ambassadors, both verbally and in diplomatic notes, that since Czechoslovakia had ceased to exist there was nothing to prevent Hungary from satisfying her claims.

It was clear to the Hungarian Government and also to the public that this favorable decision of Berlin was by no means a beautiful gesture towards Hungary, but it was rather a gesture against Poland where the population demanded that the Polish Army should occupy Ruthenian territories but which naturally would have led to disagreeable entanglements between Hungary and Rumania. On February 18 the Regent presided over a Crown Council which decided that the Honved Army Corps of Kassa should occupy within 48 hours the Ruthenian territory and ordered them to do such. The military moves which were started with approximately twenty-five thousand men went according to plan and were terminated in a few days after the annihilation and capture of the Czech units of General Prchala and the bands of the Ukrainian Szics Guardists.

The Hungarian and Polish soldiers shook friendly hands at the historical Hungarian-Polish frontier. The diplomatic circles abroad and the less informed circles in the country itself were rather surprised by the swiftness of the action taken in the settlement of the rather lengthy and drawn out negotiations of many months over the Carpatho-Ruthenian territory. But this swiftness was for good reasons. The competent Hungarian circles knew that the Czechs wanted to prevent the penetration of the Hungarian Army and that the Foreign Minister Csaky had protested such Czech intrigues in a note handed to Czech Ambassador to Budapest Kobr. Also known and threatening was that the Rumanians wanted to occupy some villages inhabited by Rumanians which were across the border and close to the city of Marmarossziget, and had concentrated troops at this sector.

The Slovaks, on the other hand, were afraid that the Hungarians would occupy some Slovakian territory also, and in order to reassure them, the Germans sent troops to the city of Eperjes [today the Slovakian Presov] which was inhabited mostly by Hungarians. Then finally there was another threat by the Ukrainian "Szics" Guardists who, under the leadership of Reverend Volosin, a priest, were organizing for armed resistance. The great speed and able tactics of the Kassa Army Corps, however, stopped all these developments in the making. Minister President Teleki immediately introduced self-government in Carpatho-Ruthenia and asked the Regent to nominate as governor administrator for the territory the outstanding, wise aristocrat with great social understanding, Baron Zsigmond Perenyi.

The Perenyi family is an old clan in the Ruthenian territory and centuries ago the fortress of Huszt was in their possession. It was very impressive to see the Ruthenians greet him when on his official travels; how they expressed their love and admiration towards him and how they kissed the seam of his robe in the old Slavic tradition. The Hungarian public was very interested in the attitudes of other countries concerning the solution of the Ruthenian problem. The Germans were somewhat skeptical. The Italians were happy. Communications reaching us from England said that a high ranking official of the Foreign Office had talked to Ambassador Barcza briefly saying only the following: "It is better that the Hungarians are in Carpatho-Ukraine than the Germans." On the other hand, the Yugoslavs acknowledged the fact without any particular comments and only the Rumanians in Bucharest were rather loud in protesting it.

Before I go into details of the diplomatic activities conducted by the Hungarians in the following two years, it seems to be necessary to give a rough outline of the general international situation developing in Europe.

I. The Munich Conference and the success of the first Berlin decisions and the indecision and impotence of London and Paris boosted to no end the self consciousness of the Third Reich. There were two slogans which were made known concerning her plans for the future: "Sud-Ostraum," which promised the spreading of German political interest in east and south-east of Europe, and the "Grossraum-Wirtschaft" which meant to subjugate this south-eastern territory and bring it into the economic sphere of the Third Reich. These political and economic plans were further strenghtened by the so-called "Stahlvertrag," or Steeltreaty, concluded in May 1939 between Berlin and Rome, which regulated the rather entangled South Tyrolean situation with its military and political sanctions, and gave a free hand to the Third Reich to realize her great German dreams. The same aims were served by a treaty concluded in August 1939 between the Third Reich and the Soviet Union, in Berlin and Moscow respectively, which comprised a series of commercial and mutual protection agreements.

The program of the Grossraum-Wirtschaft could be noted by the ever increasing pressure exercised by the Germans on the Hungarian, Rumanian, and Yugoslav production and consumption. The Sud-Ostraum political doctrines resulted in the introduction of terrorism and bloody intrigues in the Polish-German minority disputes and the dispute for the city of Danzig and the Danzig corridor. The writer of these lines often received in the mail, from both the German and Polish sides, illustrated albums showing the above mentioned brutalities. Poland, who categorically trusted English and French guarantees, refused to accede to the German demands, but even then the armed actions were not far away.

28

On September 1, 1939 German Army units penetrated the Polish Frontier, and the Blitzkrieg was started. Two days later the French and the English declared war on the Third Reich, and the Second World War began. In the middle of September the Soviet Russian Army crossed Poland's eastern frontier, occupied the so-called Ukrainian (White Russian) territories and moved down to the Carpatho-Ukrainian-Hungarian border. Preceding the Polish military moves, German Army units occupied the Slovakian Republic to secure the strategic Vienna-Pozsony-Galanta-Zsolna-Rutka railroad line. And they also started a very active anti-Hungarian propaganda in Slovakia. The German Army which penetrated Holland and Belgium forced France onto her knees, and in June 1940 concluded an armistice with the French, which split the country into an occupied territory on one side and free territory on the other. In Vichy, the Petain Government was formed.

Hitler would have liked to conclude a treaty with the British but London refused all attempts and communication. On the seas and in the air and because of the unsuccessful Italian Greek war on the Balkans, the German-English power chashes were continued.

II. Although the Italians, who were drifting with increasing speed under the influence of the Third Reich, emphasized again and again their peaceful intentions through their refusal to participate in the German-Polish war, they did conduct friendly relations with Yugoslavia and Rumania following the wishes of the Germans. Nevertheless, in April 1939, they attacked Albania with a respectable air and ground force, and after a series of ever changing tactical moves, they occupied it. Victorio Emmanuel, King of Italy, accepted the Albanian Crown. In December 1939, the Grand Council of the Fascist Party declared that it did not intend to participate in nor mingle in the German-French-English war. In spite of this, in June 1940, war was declared against France and England.

The Italian Army units, when they were unable to advance in France and in Africa because of firm counter-attacks of the English, suffered great losses on the Mediterranean. In October 1940 when it was known that Hitler had declared war on Greece, the English consequently landed on the Island of Crete and also on the Greek coast. Soon under pressure by the Greek Army, the Italians were forced to evacuate Greece. It was only the German Army, which swiftly moved down from Rumania to Bulgaria, prevented the English from occupying the entire Balkans.

III. In 1939, a new threat appeared on the European scene: the Soviet Russian Empire. We have seen already that, in spite of the English and French attempts, they had concluded a political and military pact with the Germans in August 1939. As a result of this she participated in the German-Polish war and was able to acquire Poland's Ukrainian territories. A second consequence was that in September and October, with the usual Communist methods, she was able to put her hands on the Baltic States of Estonia, Latvia, and Lithuania. These countries, made docile by their new governments, were, in the middle of 1940, incorporated into the Soviet Union.

In April 1939, the Soviet demanded frontier adjustments of Finland. The Finns refused to satisfy such claims and upon this the Red Army penetrated into Finland in spite of the sharp protests of President Roosevelt and the League of Nations. After battles in which she suffered great losses, Finland was forced to conclude peace, and Russia acquired the district of Karelia with the city of Vipurii (or Viiborg).

In the summer of 1940, the Soviet Union sent an ultimatum to Rumania requesting her to cede to Russia Bessarabia and northern Bukovina. The Rumanians were prepared to comply to this request since London had informed Bucharest that in the event of an attack by Russia on Rumania, she would not be able to support them. The two territories were consolidated under the name of Moldya and became a Russian member republic. In November of the same year Molotov, Soviet Russian Foreign Commissar, visited Berlin and exhibited a great interest in the affairs of Yugoslavia, Bulgaria, and the Dardanelles (or Bosphorus).

IV.   The value of the Hungarian relationship with London and Paris remained rather dubious. Although Czechoslovakia had ceased to exist on the map, under the leadership of Benes, the Czech emigrants, using the old connections and sympathies of England and France, developed lively political activity in the interest of the independence of Czechoslovakia. When Lord Halifax, who had little sympathy for the Hungarian cause, ceded his portfolio of Minister of Foreign Affairs to Mr. Eden, whose Czech sympathies were known, the British Government, early in 1940, officially recognized the Czechoslovakian committee and Chamberlain made a statement recommending that Czechoslovakia be reconstructed. The atmosphere in France was also favorable towards the cause of Benes, but favorable voices also were heard for the Hungarians; Count de Vienne, French Ambassador to Budapest, was sent on a secret mission to the Hungarian capital, but I will give those details later.

What were the aims of mutilated Hungary in the international political scene and in all these clashes of interests and powers which were pushing Europe to her final annihilation? All Hungary aimed to do was to keep the Hungarian nation out of all war conflicts and to reacquire the territories which were separated from her. We will see in the following how Count Pal Teleki, Minister President, and Count Istvan Csaky, Minister of Foreign Affairs, acted in the realization of these aims.

After the successful settlement of the Carpatho-Ruthenian question, Hungary withdrew from the League of Nations. Two factors brought on this decision: first, the Hungarian Government wanted to liberate herself from this absolutely impotent body and the barriers it imposed; secondly, she wanted to make a friendly gesture towards the Third Reich, who had left it earlier. The Hungarian Parliamentary circles accepted this move of the Government with great Stoicism and demonstrated little interest; the press barely mentioned it. In April 1939, the Minister President and the Minister of Foreign Affairs visited Rome. During the negotiations, which lasted only a few days, the Hungarians were left with the impression that the official communiques which stated Italy's aims to maintain peace and guarantee Yugoslavia's territorial inviclability were hiding something because Italian interests were also mentioned in Yugoslavia.

What were these interests? In the official communique the Hungarians stated that they strictly were adhering to the policies of the Axis. What was the meaning of such a statement at a time when the German-Polish relations threatened to break out into war in which the Hungarians could not get involved because of moral factors. Hungary not only did not want to participate but she was against permitting German troops to transit Hungarian territory in a move against Poland. This was the reason why Parliamentary circles received this communique with great concern, and the press gave only scarce details about it.

In these conditions, Teleki and Csaky traveled to Berlin at the end of April. The Government Party usually gave a farewell dinner at such occasions and it was the task of the writer of these lines to greet the Minister of Foreign Affairs in a speech before the Party. At his request I spoke about certain points of Hungarian foreign policy which were enveloped in a mist and upon this, in his answer, he expressed the hope that this mist be dispersed in the course of the negotiations. Verily Berlin did not insist and/or demand the use of Hungarian railroad lines leading to Poland (because apparently the Slovakian railway line mentioned previously was quite adequate for the purpose) and did not demand further government actions in connection with the Jews. However, they did request some more concessions to be granted to the Hungarian Schwabs (ethnic Germans who migrated into the country during centuries of Hapsburg rule). Apparently Rumania and Yugoslavia were not a topic of discussion at the talks but Berlin and Budapest were rather secretive about them. Ribbentropp expressed his friendly feelings towards Hungary and so did the German press.

Very shortly after their return, Csaky delivered a report to the Foreign Policy Committee of the House of Representatives giving details of the Berlin negotiations. In the course of debate Count Istvan Bethlen, former Minister President, quoted the expression used by me, "misty points," and requested further and more detailed information from the Minister. He avoided all firm statements, however, and repeatedly said that Hungary's independence is by no means limited in any respect.

After these negotiations there was every reason for the Hungarian public to be very optimistic on one side and darkly pessimistic on the other. The writer of these lines had the opportunity to talk to the Minister of Foreign Affairs for over an hour and we discussed the neutrality to be maintained by Hungary at all cost. Csaky deliberated about the possibilities and stated that there would be no war because London was going to be able to prevent such an event. Balint Homan, former Minister of Education and outstanding historian, explained at length to a very close group of friends in the presence of this author that the German "Sud-Ostraum" policy presented tremendous dangers and was a threat to Hungary's independence and her role in Europe.

It was in this rather unbalanced stage of public opinion that the Hungarian nation was informed of the treaties concluded between the Third Reich and the Soviet Union in Berlin and in Moscow, and also that Hungary had entered into diplomatic relations with Russia. Barely two weeks later the German Wehrmacht started tactical moves against Poland; and London and Paris declared war on the Third Reich.

In the gradually worsening, rather distorted European political situation which sprang out of the Munich Conference, the relationship of Hungary to her immediate neighbors was the following:

I. After the settlement of the Carpatho-Ruthenian question, provoking intrigues were felt in Slovakia. During this time the writer of these lines, being a descendent of Szekely settlers in the valley of the River Vag, often traveled about the homely countryside of the upper Hungarian territory and through many friendly conversations became convinced that the hostile attitude was not a reflection of public opinion but was a result of politics. The Deputy Foreign Minister of Slovakia Dr. Istvan Polyak, a former officer of the Hussars, an estate owner and a good friend of mine of pre-war times, communicated to me that Sanyo Mach, Slovak Minister of the Interior, was the leading spirit behind their policy and was drawing regular salary for this from the Germans. Polyak was ready to turn over to me some receipts signed by Mach.

I got another hint as to the intrigues against the Hungarians instigated by the Germans while having lunch at a hotel in the city of Trencsen. There, seated at a long table, were about fifteen or twenty young boys speaking German and being rather loud. I asked the waiter if they were Germans. He answered: "Oh, by no means. They were Slovaks who are learning German and for that they receive twenty crowns and lunch daily." Soon a gentleman at the table next to mine, came over and introduced himself as the district medical head of the county of Trencsen, and in a broken Hungarian he made the following statement: "You see what the Germans do to us; it would be

32

much better for us to learn Hungarian; and the county had made such a proposal to introduce Hungarian language courses again. We lived together for one thousand years, and we have absolutely nothing in common with the Germans."

I also had the opportunity to talk to Bela Tuka, Slovak Minister President, and to Tiszo, Secretary to President of the Slovak Republic, and both gentlemen expressed their great sympathy for the Hungarian nation; during my travels the same impression was made on me by broad sectors of the population.

II. The Hungarian Government did not cease to demand from Rumania that the territorial disputes and claims be settled on the basis of the Munich decision. The Rumanians rigidly refused to consider even the disputes or a settlement and it was also Hitler's opinion that the maintenance of peace was by all means desirable in order to secure shipments of oil and grain (cereals) undisturbed. London and Paris, on the other hand, were of the opinion that the territorial integrity of Rumania was a "European interest." Italy had no interest in Rumania, and Mussolini, as I already stated in my study entitled "Hungary and Mussolini," was inclined to support the Hungarian claims, although his voice fell on deaf ears in Berlin.

The Hungarian Government and Pal Teleki sent memorandum after memorandum elaborating on the Hungarian rights and her rightful claim to Transylvania; a tremendous amount of supporting evidence contained in several cases was shipped to London. (Those boxes somehow disappeared entirely, leaving not a trace.) In his memoirs Teleki set the Hungarian territorial claims at 78 thousand square kilometers, at the minimum, (as opposed to the 103 thousand square kilometers of territory forfeited in 1919) and presented sufficient proof and evidence that for the security of Europe it was imperative that the eastern Carpathian Mountains and their valleys be in Hungarian hands. (The evidence documenting this was transported in January 1940 to Paris and London.)

In November 1939, there came a definite turn in this series of rather lengthy debates, bargaining and negotiations when the world was informed by the Russian press that the Soviets had made claims on Bessarabia and Bukovina. It was immediately proposed by the military circles of Hungary, or at least by part of them, that the Hungarian Army should move into Transylvania and occupy the Eastern Carpathian Mountains. In the early part of January 1940, Csaky met with Ciano in Venice and asked for Ciano's support and aid in Bucharest and asked him to communicate to the Rumanians that if they would satisfy Hungary's territorial claims, Hungary would remain neutral in the event that the Soviet Union attacked Rumania. The intervention by Ciano, if it happened at all, was fruitless. As a matter of fact, Gafencu, the Rumanian Minister of Foreign Affairs, stated that Rumania had Germany as a mighty protector against the Hungarians. The Hungarian Ambassador to Berlin Sztojai reported to Budapest that if Rumanian oil fields would be threatened German armored divisions would hurry to their defense, taking the shortest route, and the Germans were already preparing some troops in eastern Slovakia for such a purpose, and it only gave incentive to the idea of an armed solution to the problem of Hungary.

Among these saber rattlings, memorandums and futile negotiations in the summer of the year 1940, the press and radio publicized that Molotov wanted to realize the claims of the Soviet Union against Rumania. Well-informed politicians also learned the top secret that Molotov had invited Kristoffy, Hungarian Ambassador to Moscow, to a talk with him and communicated to him that he wanted to support Hungary's territorial claims against Rumania. This immediately presented two new questions for the Hungarian Government to face.

What would be the Government's attitude towards the Soviet Union: to accept a sympathetic attitude seemed impossible, for there was also the threat that the Red Army would also enter into the eastern Carpathian in their advance.

What could hasten the immediate solution of the Transylvanian territorial claims? An eventual action by the Soviet Union would perhaps bury the solution of the question especially now that the new Minister President of Rumania Gigortu had renounced the friendship pact with England and France, which had guaranteed Rumania's frontiers for twenty years, and wanted to place his country under the protection of the Third Reich. Hungary under pressure of the double threat made a decisive move. After the solution of the Carpatho-Ukrainian problem, she had fortified her troops, moved them up and lined them along the Rumanian border; and now she communicated to Berlin and Rome that under the present situation she was ready to solve her problem by force of arms. Upon this Hitler invited Teleki and Csaky to Munich and there, in the presence of Ciano, the Hungarian claims were rehashed; however, it was under new light now that Teleki had threatened an armed solution; whereas King Carol of Rumania requested in a private letter to Hitler a final refusal of the Hungarian claims and the guarantee of the Rumanian frontiers. The negotiations ended with a recommendation to the Hungarian Government that it should attempt to renew negotiations and Hitler also promised that he would influence the Rumanian King to be more receptive and polite.

At this time came also a territorial claim from Bulgaria requesting from Rumania the reconstruction of her old frontiers in the Dobrudsa.

In compliance with the decision of the Munich negotiations the Hungarian Government invited the Rumanian Government to a parley. But no reply to this invitation was ever received. The Hungarian press withdrew in a great silence in order not to influence public opinion which was rather anti-Rumanian anyway. But the well-informed knew that King Carol sent a new letter to Hitler in which he offered a few thousand square kilometers of land to the Hungarians and requested that the Fuehrer should put an end to the Hungarian claims in the future and should guarantee the remaining Rumanian territory. The Hungarians, of course, declared King Carol's offers to be unacceptable and in a letter Hitler communicated to the King that he was ready to guarantee the Rumanian frontiers only if Rumania reached a final settlement with Hungary and Bulgaria on disputes.

After this the Rumanians finally made a proposal for a population exchange and in the middle of July 1940, in the city of Turnu-Severin, located on the Danube River, a Hungarian-Rumanian delegation sat down to negotiate. The Hungarian delegation was led by Andras Hory, Ambassador and Minister Plenipotentiary, and also among the members of the delegation was Laszlo Bardossy, Hungarian Ambassador who later became Minister of Foreign Affairs and Minister President. The Hungarians lived on the ship Zsofia which was in the Danube in front of the city. The negotiations were interrupted twice but ended finally without any results.

At the end of July highly informed circles learned that the Soviet Union was concentrating troops on the Rumanian border and that Molotov had communicated to Kristoffy, Hungarian Ambassador to Moscow, that he considered the Hungarian claims against Rumania well founded and just and that he was ready to support them. Moscow obviously was preparing to attack Rumania. At that time Hungary also concentrated about 400 thousand troops on the Rumanian-Hungarian border. Hitler was rather upset and excited about this news (fearing for the Rumanian oil wells), and Ribbentropp in an urgent manner, took up negotiations with Ciano in order to solicit his cooperation for settlement of the above questions and to reach a final decision.

On August 29, 1940, the two statesmen met in Vienna and there they presided over the so-called "Second Viennese Arbitrage," which I mentioned in my study entitled "Hungary and Mussolini." This "Second Viennese Arbitrage" made a bad impression on Hungarian public opinion because it brought to light the point of the so-called "Goring-Bucht;" that is to say, the very noticeable break in the tracing of the new Hungarian-Rumanian border east of Kolozsvar [Translator's remark: the present Rumanian name is Cluj]. This bay-like indentation, demanded by the Germans, behind the ancient capital of Transylvania was the site of the natural gas and oil wells of Sarmas and of several gold and alabaster mines. The decision left them in Rumanian hands. In those times I had business connections with the "Hugo Stinnes G.M.B.H., Muelheim An Der Ruhr," a German finance concern which was third in their nation after Krupp

and Goring-Werke, and I maintained friendly relations with its
head, Hugo Stinnes. He realted to me the history of this "Goring-
Bucht." [Translator's remark: Goring-Bucht means Goring
Bay] Gigurtu, the Rumanian Minister President, was personally
interested in the economic exploitation of the above territory
and should this territory come under Hungarian rule he would
lose a noticeable income. Therefore, he offered to the German
Government the business firms working in the territory. The
German Government channeled the offer over to the Goring-
Werke and Stinnes GMBH financial concern for further negotiation and finalization. The Stinnes concern only received the
invitation of the German Government quite late and thus,
missed the opportunity. Hugo Stinnes added to his statements:
"Believe me, Mr. Baross, if we would have been the purchasers,
this territory would not have stayed with the Rumanians."

Out of gratitude to the Third Reich and its cooperation with
the settlement of the Transylvanian territorial disputes, the
Hungarian Government gave far concessions to the Hungarian
and Transylvanian ethnic German groups and allowed them
to enter into the "Volks Bund der Deutschen in Ungarn," which
was an organization directly under the influence of the Third
Reich, renewed the privilege of the use of their language
(which had never been barred to them), expressed again that
they were equal to Hungarians in public office (this had never
been disputed) and that if they had changed their German
name to a Hungarian one, they were allowed to change it back.
Another expression of gratitude, or at least the press interpreted
it as one, was that in November Hungary joined the signatories
to the German-Italian-Japanese Tripartite treaty. The international political consequence of this was that the Third Reich
gained confidence in Hungary, and the domestic political consequence was that the German Government seemed to decrease
her support to ethnic German and right wing movements in
the country.

Once the Rumanian troops had ceded the Transylvanian
territories, following exactly the stipulation of the negotiations,
Hitler communicated to the Rumanian King that he was guar-
anteeing the new frontiers. A few weeks later Carol abdicated
and ceded his throne to his son, Michael. The Rumanian Government also abdicated and Gigurtu was replaced by General
Antonescu, and these changes shifted the entire Rumanian
policy and political life over to the German line. After this,
upon advice of Hitler, Rumania also ceded the northern parts
of Bukovina and Bessarabia to the Soviet Union, and the Soviet
troops immediately occupied the said territory. Bulgaria regained from Rumania the Dobrudsa frontier lines of 1918.

In the meantime, German Army units moved into Rumania
to secure and defend the oil wells. (These troops were sent in
great secret in locked railroad cars also through Hungary.)

III.   In my study entitled "Hungary and Mussolini," I traced the development of the Hungarian-Yugoslav relationship and I also included that in December 1940, Foreign Minister Csaky had concluded a pact in Belgrade in which Hungary and Yugoslavia pledged "eternal peace and friendship" to each other. I also mentioned that territorial questions which had arisen between the two countries were postponed to a later date by common agreement of the negotiating parties. They reached an understanding that the secret purpose of this pact was really to counter-balance the steadily increasing influence of the Third Reich. The secret negotiation was conducted by Csaky, the Regent Prince Paul, who ruled until the King of Yugoslavia came of age, and Minister President Cvethovic. The German Government received the news of the Hungarian-Yugoslav pact with great satisfaction (the newspapers did not cease to praise the wisdom of the Hungarian Government) because it apparently agreed with their desire for peace in the Balkans. The Italians also seemed happy although at the time they had secret plans for Croatia and Dalmatia, but we did receive unfavorable news from London.

The British strongly disapproved of our having signed the Tripartite Pact [Translator's remark: Anti-comintern pact of Germany, Italy, and Japan], and also it upset them that we had tolerated the transportation of German troops, although in a secret way, to Rumania. They also charged us with wanting to shift the Yugoslavs into German influence with our Belgrade pact. Although according to statements made by Gyorgy Barcza, Hungarian Ambassador to London, that the English opinion changed later, the English attitude of un-comprehension had aroused great ire in Hungary and had caused Pal Teleki, Minister President, to become quite excited about it. Those persons close to him observed with great concern his tired and nervous condition.

The German Government, in reality, tried to pressure the Government of Yugoslavia to adhere to the Tripartite Treaty. The Hungarian Government received this with great anxiety because it feared that in the course of the negotiations the Germans would make promises to Belgrade to guarantee their frontiers. This would have endangered the validity of some allowances made to Foreign Minister Csaky in regard to some territorial claims. After long hesitation, the Yugoslav Minister President signed the Tripartite Pact in the last days of March 1941, at Vienna, and the Third Reich immediately announced that it was going to "observe forever the territorial integrity and independence of Yugoslavia." However, she did not guarantee the frontiers against Hungarian or other claims.

Two days later, however, the situation changed radically. The Soviet Union arranged a political coup d'état which removed Prince Regent Paul from the throne and placed the seventeen year old Peter II on it instead, and set up a government under the leadership of General Simovics who immediately concluded a friendship pact with Moscow.

Count Istvan Csaky did not live to know about this turn of events. On January 27, after great suffering, he died of a kidney ailment which he had contracted in a French prison camp during the First World War. This ailment flared up again during the negotiations in Belgrade and soon killed him. His successor was Laszlo Bardossy, Hungarian Ambassador to London and later to Bucharest. It was he who had to face all the increasing difficulties.

The unfortunate military ventures of Italy in Albania and Greece finally resulted in a complete rout of the Italian Army on all fronts. The English hurried to the aid of the two attacked countries and they landed on the Island of Crete and in Greece proper, united with the Greek Army and started to advance towards Bulgaria. Ribbentropp gathered from Molotov in the cause of previous negotiations that the Soviet Union, continuing the Czarist politics, also coveted the Bosphorus and would have liked to have the Balkans within her sphere of interest. The coup d'état of Belgrade seemed to indicate that already the country had been thrown into the arms of the Soviets. Under these circumstances, Hitler resolved to a series of ruthless forceful measures. As an introduction he sent German troops from Rumania to occupy Bulgaria.

A few hours after the coup d'état in Belgrade, the German and the Italian Governments warned the Yugoslav Government in a mutual note that they considered the change in government a breach of the Tripartite Pact and would not tolerate it. At the same time the German Government communicated to the Hungarian Government that she intended to use force of arms against Yugoslavia and expressed the hope that Hungary would participate also in the military moves and it seemed advisable that the Hungarian and German general staffs meet to negotiate the details. The Hungarian Government was not surprised by this secret dispatch, because the German Third Reich had lauded the Hungarian Yugoslav friendship pact so highly, but had not expected her to insist upon military intervention. The Government had hoped that it would satisfy the Germans to insist upon crossing Hungarian territory to reach Yugoslavia. Therefore, it was a very disagreeable surprise to learn after the meeting of the German and Hungarian general staffs that the Germans had demanded that several (five, if I remember well) army corps participate in the tactical moves. Pal Teleki categorically refused to accede to this demand, but the Regent, and also the majority of the Cabinet members and broad circles of the Houses of Parliament, thought it desirable and necessary that Hungarian forces participate. They reasoned, and not without grounds, that if the Wehrmacht alone occupied the old Southern Hungarian territories, they might eventually be lost forever from us, especially since the ethnic German settlers of these southern territories had wanted to form an independent "Prinz Eugen Gau" administrative territory out of former Bacska and Banat and also even of the pure Hungarian counties of Baranya and Tolna. This territory would be under the direct rule of the Third Reich. Finally the Crown Council, with the Regent presiding, released three army corps to the disposal of the Germans, sent the fourth army corps to the Hungarian Russian border to hold a protective defense position, and it also set up the condition that all troops would not cross the former Hungarian-Croatian and Hungarian-Serbian frontiers and that their tactical moves were limited to exclusively Hungarian territories, that is to say, the Bacska and Banat.

All the above happenings were brought to the attention of the English Government by Pal Teleki in hopes that they would be understanding of the attitude of the Hungarian Government. But within a few hours London replied through Gyorgy Barcza, the Hungarian Ambassador, to the Hungarian Government that if it were going to allow the transporting of German troops through Hungarian territory, diplomatic relations would be broken off with them, and that if we were going to grant armed assistance to the Third Reich, war would be declared on Hungary. On the morning of April 3, 1941, Pal Teleki was found dead in his bed. He had shot himself. Among the letters which he left behind, there was one addressed to the Regent. Some sentences are quoted here in fragments: "We became traitors. I allowed the nation to lose her honor; maybe I am doing a service through my suicide to my country." This letter was never publicized but these few words were quoted to me by a very good friend of mine Dr. Peter Incze, personal secretary to Pal Teleki and counselor to the Minister Presidency.

In the afternoon of the same day, the Regent entrusted the duties of Minister President to Laszlo Bardossy. Bardossy also kept the portfolio of Minister of Foreign Affairs.

The same day Hugo Stinnes, who happened to be staying in Budapest, visited me and expressed his great sympathy concerning the tragic death of Pal Teleki and he was quite pale in the face when he added: "Hoffentlich kein Wechsel es ware furchterlich..." [Translator's remark: English: "I am hopeful that there is not going to be any change, it would be terrible..."] This remark of the reserved and cold businessman surprised me and at the same time made me very afraid. It remained in my memory.

While the bloodless body of Pal Teleki was reposing in its sarcophagus at the Minister Presidency, the armored cars, cannons, and armored infantry of the Wehrmacht hurried in endless columns day and night down along the River Danube on both sides, in Buda and in Pest. It would be interesting to know how many of the thousands of people who watched this phenomena were thinking that such a tremendous military force could have annihilated the entire country at only one stroke of the hand.

In five consecutive years the nation had mourned over the death of Gyula Gombos, Kalman Daranyi (the latter died of a heart attack and an embolus in the brain), Istvan Csaky, and Pal Teleki. This is one of the most tragic chapters of the Hungary story, for with the passing away of these great personalities, the nation lost men of outstanding leadership and ability. These men had had a great and deep concept of a future for Hungary which was based on the reconstruction of the historical Hungary and its modernization. Although there were shades of differences in their policies, all four of them tried to realize their plans with equal purposefulness, heroism, and self sacrifice within the great cataracts of European and world currents of history. Their thoughts and their deeds were guided exclusively by the interest of the nation. They lived for it and they actually died for it because their deaths came while they were serving their nation.

The Armies of the Third Reich moved up along the frontiers of Yugoslavia passing through Hungary, Austria, Bulgaria, and Rumania. In the morning of April 6, the German and Italian Governments in a renewed mutual note communicated to the Yugoslav Government that they considered the Balkans in their sphere of interest, that they were not going to tolerate any kind of entanglements there, and that they declared the Belgrade coup d'état a hostile act against the Tripartite Alliance. A few hours later the German Army penetrated Yugoslavia from all sides and started her tactical moves. During this time, the Hungarian Government continued to negotiate with the Germans. In spite of the mentioned decisions of the Crown Council, Bardossy was confident that eventually the Germans would be satisfied with a smaller force of the Honved, and he was afraid that if he lent larger military force to the Wehrmacht it might be taken farther into the Balkans. Bardossy insisted that the Honved Army occupy only the Bacska and Banat, the old Hungarian territories, and by no means should step over the historical Hungarian-Serb, and Hungarian-Croatian frontiers respectively. Finally he requested that the Honved Army should begin tactical moves only when Yugoslavia ceased to exist. The Regent and Hitler exchanged letters and the Hungarian generals (among them Bartha, Minister of Defense, and Werth) negotiated with German generals in Berlin (among them Paulus and Keitl) and the result of the negotiations in Budapest was a mutual understanding that about four or five divisions of the Hungarian Army would participate in the moves, and would occupy the Bacska and the Banat and would leave the old Serb and Croatian frontiers intact.

On April 7, the English Air Force bombed some Hungarian cities and the English Ambassador to Budapest communicated to the Hungarian Government that England was severing diplomatic relations with Hungary. On April 10, Croatia and Slavonia declared their independence and with that Yugoslavia ceased to exist. On April 12, the Hungarian Honved divisions began their tactical moves. On April 15, F.D. Roosevelt, President of the United States, officially recognized the Hungarian attack on Yugoslavia, and in spite of the protests of the Hungarian Ambassador in Washington, declared that the United States and its citizens unanimously joined in condemning this action by the Hungarians.

The Hungarian Honved units continued their tactical moves according to plan. One division penetrated the so-called Baranya Triangle, which was a territory located at the junction of the Rivers Danube and Drava, which had belonged once to the county of Baranya, but then was detached and given to Yugoslavia in 1919. The troops were not met with armed resistance. Three other divisions moved into the Bacska, that is to say, in the old county of Bacs-Bodrog, and after having broken through three lines of defense, they meticulously followed the Croatian frontier line and reached the Danube River. The Hungarian and German population of the territories greeted the Hungarian Honved Army with great joy and a Serb battalion joined them even. But the Banat, consisting of the former Hungarian counties of Temes, Arad, and Torontal, was never occupied because Bucharest was against turning these territories over to the Hungarians; therefore, the Germans occupied them and the decision about the annexation of the territory was postponed. This German attitude toward the cancellation of previous agreements (very much like that of the "Goring-Bucht" [Translator's remark: Goring Bay]) was very disappointing for Hungary, and caused great animosity; it became obvious that this had been a gesture towards the Rumanians and that Pan-Germanic supporters had a hand in it.

With the cessation of military moves, the reorganization of the occupied territories was taken over by the military administration and the peaceful and friendly atmosphere of the Bacska changed and became very much distorted. Sectors of the Serb population obtained weapons somehow and started partisan "Komitachi" activities and raids against Hungarian soldiers and gendarmery outposts. The soldiers did not like being shot at from houses and gulches, and these acts of terrorism sadly enough led to some very severe and bloody retaliation. The Hungarian Government resettled about thirty to forty thousand Serbs, partly voluntarily and partly through Government force, from this part of the territory and settled in their place Hungarian minorities from the Rumanian Moldva who are called Csango.

Under the leadership of the Kvaternik and the President Pavelics, Croatia became a republic, and the Hungarian Government recognized it immediately. The Hungarian-Croatian relationships, which had been very friendly at the start, soon ran into the difficulty over the territory located between the rivers Drava and Mura.

With the termination of the military moves of the Wehrmacht in Serbia, Hugo Stinnes asked me to travel on his behalf to Sophia, the capital of Bulgaria, to settle certain coal negotiations and disputes with the Bulgarians. I was very happy to do such for I had become very much interested in the Balkan situation and I wanted to study it first hand. I traveled by the Orient Express, and although it usually made the Belgrade-Sofia trip in six hours, it took fifty hours this time because the railroad line was under control of the Serb partisans and the Express had armored cars and cars manned with machine gun personnel to grant it protection and a free road. Although my trip was undisturbed, every railroad bridge and tunnel represented a major military project and the whole surrounding area had to be searched with a fine tooth comb; therefore, the train was forced to stop for hours and wait for a signal to proceed.

Everywhere in Sofia, in the street, in the offices, or in the shops, I was asked, "Are you a German?" When I would say that I was a Hungarian, they became very friendly and immediately started to make sarcastic remarks about the Germans who were everywhere in the city and country. If I remember well, a very high German naval command had its headquarters in Sofia, and there were innumerable German officers in the hotel. I observed the forced smiles of the Bulgarians when they were talking to these men. They very often asked me if I spoke either French or English, and upon my affirmative answer, they would immediately switch over to these languages although they spoke perfect German.

In those times there were very severe battles being fought in Greece and Albania. The Balkans were nothing but a big powder keg.

In spring of the year 1941, a shortage of public alimentation became perceptible. The needs of the Hungarian Army, mobilized for the tactical moves in the south, increased the demand for food shipments over and above those which were to be sent to the Third Reich in compliance with previous economic negotiations and agreements. The Government introduced measures which were characteristic of the First World War. It introduced a new food rationing which, of course, was met with great dissatisfaction everywhere in the country.

As I already mentioned, in November 1940, Molotov, Foreign Affairs Commissar of the Soviet Union, made hints as to the interest of Moscow in Yugoslavia, Bulgaria, and the Bosphorus. The Soviet Russian Empire obviously wanted to continue the centuries old Balkan policy of the Czars and this fact did not surprise anybody in Hungary. The Hungarians remembered well the circumstances which surrounded the First World War and the attitudes of the Czars in it. The Hungarians also saw a definite change in the situation of the Balkans; there the

42

intrigues of the Czarist Pravoslav and Panslavic elements were taken over by the Soviet Russian Communist imperialistic policies of expansion. At the same time the able Austrian, Hungarian, English, French, and Turkish diplomats were substituted now by the ruthless and tremendous military force of the Third Reich. There was no question that the competition of the two imperialistic tendencies can be solved only through a war.

A terrible question arose immediately: what will be the fate and the role of Hungary in this inevitable clash of powers?

As early as March 1941, President Bardossy and the Hungarian General Staff had been notified by Berlin that Moscow was conducting a double faced policy. Berlin wanted this situation clarified all the more, for the Russians had moved and concentrated a tremendous military force along the German eastern front lines. The press was silent about these messages, but both parliamentary and military circles were cognizant of them. The meetings of the Hungarian and German General Staff became more frequent and news gathered about them seemed to indicate that Berlin was not requesting Hungary's participation in tactical moves against the Communists, but wanted us to defend our Carpathian frontiers. To this end our Eighth Army Corps, located in Kassa, and the Mountaineer and Ranger Batallions were brought up to combat readiness, and they were all moved in to defense positions in the Carpathian Mountains. Several times, in confidential circles and in front of the writer of these lines, Bardossy hinted that he did not intend to grant any military assistance to the Germans. He stated further that, upon his proposal, one of the Council of Ministers brought a decision to this effect; at the same time it was decided to defend the Carpathian frontier and lend, in case of need, technical support only for the German tactical moves. The Regent fully approved of this decision of the Cabinet.

On June 22 of the year 1941 (this tragic date is carved in my memory forever), approximately 170 German Divisions, without any previous declaration of war, started their attack against the Soviet Russian Empire.

Five days later, on the 27th of July, Bardossy declared in the Lower House of Parliament that we entered a phase of war with the Soviet Russians. At the same time a similar statement was made by the President of the Upper House to the members of that chamber.

What could have caused such a cardinal change in the attitude of the Hungarian Government? I am giving here the most important and decisive factors:

I. It was an open secret that General Henrik Werth, Chief of Staff of the Hungarian General Staff, and our Ambassador to Berlin, Dome Sztojai, had submitted several memorandums which stated their opinions on Hungarian participation in the German moves. Their advice to the Hungarian Government was that, in spite of the fact that the Third Reich had not requested the armed participation of Hungary in the warfare against Soviet Russia, it appeared to be both right and unavoidable that we should elect to do so on our own initiative. They gave several reasons for supporting this recommendation and emphasized that the German Army would vanquish the Red Army in six weeks.

II.   At first the Regent and Bardossy were not inclined to take this proposition and advice into consideration. Later, under the influence of an enthusiastic and private letter from Hitler, in which the start of tactical moves on the part of the Wehrmacht was mentioned, the Regent apparently changed his opinion. In the same letter Hitler spoke about a "Crusade" against the Communists. This may have induced the Regent to talk of such a crusade to his Entourage and may consequently have moved Bardossy to look at such an action as a necessity also. The slogan "Crusade" spread like brush fire all over the country.

III.   The Finns, the Italians, and the Rumanians declared war on the Soviet Union and at the same time the Wehrmacht started its attack. Slovakia was soon to follow suit.

IV.   On the 26th of June, three Russian airplanes bombed the city of Kassa causing some damage to the city. This air raid may have warranted a declaration of war. I have to mention, however, that Colonel Geza Krudy, the commander of the anti-aircraft defense of Kassa, reported on the next day that one of the airplanes shot down bore certain yellow colored markings which would indicate that the airplanes may not have been Russian, but camouflaged German planes. This question was never clarified, and it is a fact that both the Russians and the Germans equally denied the attack. In spite of the lengthy explanations of the press, the Hungarian public opinion still did not see clear whether this provocation was a Russian or a German one.

V.   Hungary, because of her geographical location, was in the middle of the German and Russian military moves and thus could not risk being merely a passive on-looker in this armed clash. Such an attitude would have led sooner or later to merciless drastic German actions, similar to those which happened without fail three years later.

VI.   Upon evaluating the situation, every thinking man in Hungary was well aware of the fact that the declaration of war on the Soviet Union would lead to a declaration of war on Hungary by both England and the United States. Finding a practical solution to such a possibility seemed, however, to be very futile, even to those who doubted the ultimate victory of the Germans.

No matter how we evaluate these happenings in retrospect, it seems very logical to state that in consideration of the weight and value of the situation, Hungary was not in the position to avoid such a declaration of war. First of all, Hungary was a signatory to the Anti-Commintern Pact and after the Finnish,

44

Italian, Rumanian, and Slovakian declarations of war, she would have been brought into an impossible foreign political situation with these strong allies. Secondly, she had to take into consideration the immediate actions of the Third Reich, actions of retaliation, against which she was not prepared politically or militarily. The nation always carried a traditional hatred against both the Germans and the Russians. But when these feelings were weighed, the scale dipped toward the Russians.

Bardossy, with prior authority from the Regent, requested the consent of the Council of Ministers for this declaration of war. This represents a point of contention, however, for the Regent later denied having given Bardossy any such authority. Other personalities, however, maintained that the Regent not only gave "Authority" but direct "Order" to Bardossy. Although the Council of Ministers gave their consent for the declaration of war, their decision was preceded by very heated debate. As Vitez Ferenc Keresztes-Fischer, Minister of the Interior, told me himself, he opposed it very vehemently and moved that the Council should adopt an attitude of waiting and of postponement. Bardossy made his announcement in the Parliament with the consent of the Council of Ministers but through this action he should have set aside that stipulation of the Hungarian Constitution that all declarations of war be approved by the Hungarian Parliament first. The omission of this very important step was not observed at that time or noticed by anybody, not even by the leaders of the Socialist Opposition Party. Both Houses of Parliament acknowledged the news of the declaration of war with enthusiasm. In the interest of true historical description, I must point out that this enthusiasm was not limited to Parliamentary circles only. The population of the country itself, without any differentiation as to rank or profession was adhering to it. In the course of my visits and my conversations at various political clubs, I was able to observe that in Parliamentary circles they debated only one question; "To what extent the Hungarian military forces should participate?" Some proposed that the entire Hungarian Army should be sent to the front. Others would have been satisfied with only a mobilization of a few divisions, as a gesture. The press, of course, was overly enthusiastic, which was absolutely unnecessary. In the country the farmers feverishly worked on the harvest and the storing of the same, to enable them to join their units in case such a move was necessitated by the speed up of mobilization. The workers of the war industry and industrial plants were performing their duties with no less zeal and diligence. Those few who because of their Communistic or Pan-Slavistic attitudes did not participate in this enthusiasm (according to my observations, there were even such elements in the highest circles of aristocracy in the country) hid their feelings to the public. In the following very grave and burdensome four years, I traveled all over the country as a private

45

citizen and latter as a soldier, nowhere did I find bitter opposition or sabotage actions. On the contrary, I learned of many great sacrifices which were far, far above the duties of a nation at war. Therefore, I am branding a lie all those statements made by certain Hungarian elements which refer to "camouflaged resistance" or "successful sabotage attempts." They are made-up tales serving individual egocentric purposes,

There is one episode that should be mentioned, however. In those times an organization called "The Popular Front" was quickly talked about. The members of this organization were recruited from the circles of the intelligentsia and conducted a war against "Dictatorships," "Bloodshed," and "Nationalism," and were talking of "Enlightened Liberalism." They did not cause any disturbance as far as the public was concerned, and little was made of the fact that the Minister of the Interior had some of the loudest members incarcerated. Only many years later in the emigration did we learn that a few Communist agents successfully played a role in this Popular Front organ. These agents came home from Moscow during the periods of Hungarian-Russian fraternization, and they are still playing a role in Hungary's public life.

The Hungarian tactical moves were introduced with an air raid conducted into the territory of Stanislaw. I mentioned previously that on the Carpatho-Ukrainian Frontier our Ranger and Mountaineer divisions took stand, and behind them the Eighth Army Corps of Kassa. This was the so-called "Carpathian Group." The commanding officer was Major General Ferenc Szombathelyi, who also led the tactical moves in the Bacska. The "Carpathian Group" started its advancing on June 28 against an overpoweringly numerous Soviet Army. I don't think it is necessary to give details here of the tactical moves of the Hungarian armed forces and I am going to mention only those which have a relation to the political happenings. In the course of very heavy fighting the attack in Stanislaw developed into a great success. In the first days of the month of July, our army units had reached and, in some instances, crossed the River Dnyester. Here the Eighth Army Corps, transformed into a quick moving cavalry corps, was integrated into the Seventeenth German Army. The Ranger and Alpine divisions were thrown into action against enemy units roaming in the occupied territories.

The above mentioned army corps was fighting on the southern wing of the German Army. After heavy losses it reached the River Bug in the first days of August and, crossing it, made its way in the course of the month of September to the River Dnyeper and in October to the Donyec River Region.

In the meantime two important things happened in Budapest. The Regent removed, in the beginning of September, the Chief of Staff, General Werth, from his position and nominated to his place Major General Ferenc Szombathelyi, the commanding officer of the Hungarian Expeditionary Army at the front. The cause of this very surprising change in command, as explained by well-informed military circles (from whom I obtained my information), was the fact that the Regent felt that the ever increasing military requests of Werth were largely exaggerated. He accepted rather the sound advice which Szombathelyi sent him in form of a memorandum. The report contained evaluation of his experiences on the front, and advised caution and measure in the actions. Also, in the month of September, the Regent, Bardossy, and Szombathelyi traveled to the General Headquarters of Hitler to conduct talks about military questions. There the Hungarians tried to throw light on three very important points arising out of the situation. First, the Hungarian Honved Army had inadequate equipment and arms and could hardly be used for decisive tactical moves. The second point was that in the vast territories behind the front, partisan units were active and threatening all lines of supply. Point three, that the Hungarian Army units on the front should be eventually utilized for combating partisan activities. Although the Germans accepted the Hungarian standpoint they immediately demanded more wheat and oil from Hungary. In the course of the conversation they also touched on the Banat question, but the settlement of this was postponed by Hitler to a later date.

Much had already been heard about these partisan activities in the first five months of the war. I have already mentioned that in Serbia, Royalist and Communist elements were bitterly fighting the Germans and each other. In Rumania, because of the political moves introduced by General Antonescu and the terror actions of the brown shirted "Iron Guard" of Horia Sima, the mistrust increased day by day against the Germans. The Germans, however, did not recognize the danger of the "Powder Kegs" of the Balkans and ignored the anti-German feelings and hatred growing the new Croatian Republic, which was organized under the presidency of Ante Pavelics. In Slovakia the Germans instigated against the Hungarians but did not notice that large circles were listening to the radio broadcasts of BBC and openly cursing the "Nyemci." A very peculiar situation developed in the former Austrian Galicia which lays north of our Carpathian frontiers. There, Polish and Ukrainian partisans fought the Germans and they quite often drifted into Hungarian territory where they destroyed exclusively German war material and very willingly and enthusiastically supported Hungarian units in their fights against the Russians. Similar was the situation in southern part of the Soviet Empire, in the Ukrainian territories where the population first sympathized greatly with the "Liberators" but when the latter introduced senseless measures against the "Ukrainian National Movement" their partisans started to threaten the German supply lines also. These units soon formed partisan bases and cooperated with Russian units.

In compliance with the agreement reached in September at the German Headquarters the Hungarian Cavalry Corps and the two divisions which were sent to its reinforcements were used in fighting partisans in the territories of Reumahtorovkq and Brjansk. These tactical moves were developed according to plans in the first part of the year 1942, but in the fatally deteriorating political and military situation, they created tremendous new burdensome problems for Hungary.

Point 1. Already in the last days of November 1941, the British communicated with the Hungarian Government that, if it did not withdraw its troops from the eastern front and if it did not cease tactical moves against Soviet Russia till December 5, Britain was going to consider the English-Hungarian relationship as that of a state of war. We could not comply with the requests of the English and we didn't want to because we considered the fight against the Communists a national interest and a duty over and above our obligations to our allies. Thus we entered a state of war with England. At the same time London declared war on Finland and Rumania.

Point 2. In the first days of December 1941, Hungary heard of the sneak attacks of the Japanese on Pearl Harbor and of the war declared on the United States. This move was immediately followed by a declaration of war by the Third Reich and by Italy. The German Ministry of Foreign Affairs hurried to inform Sztojai, our Ambassador at Berlin, that it was expected that Hungary was going to follow the example. Bardossy was very disagreeably surprised and affected by the expression of such a German "Hope" and, as he explained it in confidential circles, he hoped to be able to avoid a direct declaration of war on the United States through merely stating that Hungary was in hostile relationship with that country. The Berlin Government, however, and also, under its pressure, the Italians, referring to our obligations as stipulated in the Tripartite Pacts, demanded a declaration of war stating that Rumania and Bulgaria had already done so. In this precarious and forced situation, Bardossy with the consent of the Council of Ministers communicated in writing to the Chargé d'Affaires of the United States at Budapest, the declaration of war on behalf of Hungary. Again violating the Constitution, he reported this action to the Houses of Parliament after the fact.

Point 3. Also in the month of December Hitler removed General Von Brauchitsch of his chief command of the German Army and reserved this power to himself. The reason for the removal of this outstanding German General was that Von Brauchitsch wanted to annihilate the Russian Soviet Army in decisive tactical moves in the Moscow region, whereas Hitler wanted to occupy, above all, the oil fields beyond the Caucasian Mountains. This strategic aim, as we will see it later, caused the complete loss of the war. The Hungarian Chief Command recognized this fact and the Chief of Staff, Ferenc Szombathelyi, still as the commander of the "Carpathian Group" hinted to such possibility in his memorandum mentioned previously in this text by stating: "The times of the Blitzkreig are over." A similar report was written and submitted verbally to the Regent by the Commander of the 2nd Hungarian Army, General Gusztav Jany. At a social gathering he whispered to the writer of these lines: "Absolutely nothing is going well."

Hitler in the beginning of January 1942, sent a private letter to Horthy, in which he requested an increase in the number of Hungarian Honveds at the battlefields, and it is quite obvious that this was a consequence of the ever deteriorating situation at the front. A few days later, Ribbentropp, participating at a hunting party, stated that a "general mobilization" would be desirable. In the last days of the same month, General Keitel, the Chief of Staff of the German General Staff, arrived at Budapest with a numerous suite and demanded directly the utilization of the entire Hungarian Army. The negotiations, according to news fragments reaching the outside world, were very stormy. The Hungarians, referring to the inadequate equipment and training of the army, the unreliability of their neighbors, and the fact that a reserve had to be kept for the defense of the country proper, at first refused any increase in the number of the Expeditionary Army. After difficult and lenghty negotiations, an agreement was reached according to which the Hungarian Government was going to mobilize the Third Army Corps of Szombathelyi, the Fourth Corps of Pecs, and the Seventh Corps of Miskolc. These units, after being adequately equipped by the Germans and having received training were to be turned over to the disposition of the German High Command. These became the Second Hungarian Army, the commandership of which was entrusted by the Regent to General Gusztav Jany. It has to be mentioned that this renewed sacrifice brought by the Hungarians was not rewarded at this time either by the settlement of the question of the return of the Banat territory. The Fifth Army Corps of Szeged, the Sixth Corps of Debrecen and the Ninth Corps of Kolozsvar remained in the country as defensive reserve.

Only five weeks later, a very important happening influenced Hungarian internal and foreign policy in a decisive manner. The Regent relieved Laszlo Bardossy of his position as Minister President and entrusted the Prime Minister's task to Miklos Kallay. To this day the reasons for the removal of Bardossy are not quite clear. Some are of the opinion that the question of the substitution of the temporarily ailing Regent may have been the cause. Well-informed Parliamentary circles and persons usually reliable agreed that a substitution of the Head of State in such critical times was eminently important and had to be provided for. The consensus was that this was a constitutional question to be regulated in form of a law and that the son of the Regent, Istvan Horthy, should be nominated for the position of Deputy Regent, to be elected by the Houses of Parliament.

The opinions diverged only on one point; whether in the law there should be a provision for a Deputy Regent or for a Deputy Regent and Successor. Bardossy originally wanted to submit a proposition to the Houses of Parliament to elect a Deputy and not a Successor. With this stand he invited the ire of the Regent, and many saw this removal as an out come of this. On the other hand, other well-informed circles felt that the Regent was very critical of the rather weak attitudes of Bardossy against the ever more powerful extremist right wing movements. There were others, like myself, who thought that he acquired many enemies by his abrupt and sometimes very rude manners. Officially he resigned because of his conditions of health.

The appointment of Kallay was a great surprise because many thought him not capable of answering the requirements of a Minister Presidential position. In the eyes of the general public he was a "Gentry from Szabolcs County," a friendly, very witty gentleman, without experience, scientific background, or the decisive power necessary to cope with the rather responsible tasks of a Prime Minister. Kallay took over his office in the first days of March of the year 1942 and temporarily reserved for himself the portfolio of the Minister of Foreign Affairs also. Not until July of the year 1943 did he relinquish this latter position to the Deputy Foreign Minister, Jeno Ghiczy. The political era which began with his entry into office was stamped by the satirists after a Hungarian folk dance, the "Kallay Double." Kallay originated from an ancient Hungarian family, a family which came into the country a thousand years ago at its occupation. As a member of such a clan, his hatred towards the Germans was obvious, as well as his great sympathy towards the English and his disinterested attitude in social questions. Political circles looked with interest and great anxiety at his next moves in setting these factors to work in the rather entangled situation of the internal and external political life of the country.

Kallay started his internal political activities by inviting the attention of the public through all information media to the fact that he was a Minister of Agriculture under Gombos and that he was going to follow with unshaken loyalty those political trends. He also made it clear that he was linked to Bardossy with a warm friendship, that their opinions were common, and that his political trends were going to be characterized by relentless national feelings. In a brilliant introductory speech at the meeting of the Government Party he gave details about his future plans emphasizing his firm adherence to the policies of the "Axis". Unquestionably the statements of Kallay made a very great impression on the country especially since their honesty was supported by the nomination of several strongly nationalist personalities to positions of confidence. In foreign political respects, his beginning was much less auspicious. The German news media received him with rather icy disinterest. In

May 1942, England concluded an alliance with Soviet Russia and even communicated to Benes that it regarded the First Viennese decision void. The Italians informed Kallay that they could receive him only after he visited Hitler. Antonescu, Rumanian Minister President, vehemently attacked Hungary in one of his Parliamentary speeches and news of great demonstrations at which they were demanding the extension of the Rumanian frontiers to the Tisza River was disseminated. Similarly,, heated attacks were directed against us in the Croatian Sabor, the national assembly. The United States communicated with the Hungarian Government and other satelite countries at the same time through our representation in Switzerland. The United States did not want to use force of arms against us because we were participating in the war against the Russian Soviet Empire only under duress. Upon this communication Kallay stated that: we entered the war on our own because of a sneak attack of the Russians directed against the town of Kassa.

After lengthy delays Miklos Kallay, upon invitation, visited Hitler at his East Prussian Headquarters. Apparently in the course of the negotiations the hostile attitude of the Rumanians was brought up and Hitler stated that he did not have anything against the Hungarians attacking Rumania after the war, but at the same time mentioned that: "The Rumanians are better soldiers than the Hungarians" and that at the present time he did not want to mingle in Rumanian internal affairs. Also the Jewish question was brought up, however, without new demands on the part of Hitler. Furthermore, the question of the Volksdeutsch was discussed and Hitler asked the approval of the Hungarian Government to a recruitment into the SS of about 30,000 Hungarians who were of German extraction, reasoning that Germans everywhere in the world should participate in the heroic struggle of the Third Reich. Shortly after this, the Volksbund, functioning in Hungary, started drafting these people, but the icy attitude of Berlin against the Kallay government remained unchanged. Pretty soon, in the month of October, the Jewish question flared up again. The German Ambassador at Budapest transmitted a note to the Hungarian Government in which the immediate and thorough exclusion of the Jews from public and economic life, a designation of them with a yellow star, and also an organization for their expatriation was demanded. Also the German demands as to food supplies and articles of consumption were increased: Against these the Third Reich promised to deliver industrial products and coal.

In those times, in the second part of the year 1942, rumors had already started about the development of links to England and to the United States by Kallay. These twains led through Lisbon, Madrid, and Ankara, and, of course, were densely enveloped in the veils of strict secrecy. I obtained information concerning these moves from such acquaintances as Andras Mecser, Bela Marton, and others, who frequently visited Germany. This clearly shows that these machinations were by no means secret to the Third Reich. Only many years later in the emigration did I acquire more information about the methods and their results in connection with these. Everybody, however, who kept their eyes open could see the definite change in the attitudes of the government toward the Germans. Kallay declared in the Foreign Affairs Committee of the Parliament that Hungary was fighting against Soviet Empire only and did not want to fight the other enemies of the Axis. The German and Italian Governments demanded a declaration of war against Chile, but the Hungarian Government refused to accede. No measures were introduced for the settlement of the Jewish question. Furthermore, neither the manifestations of the left wing parties and social organizations against the Germans nor towards the English and the U.S.A. were stopped. The general public, obviously influenced by news media disseminated by government agencies, regardless of political opinion, started to demand the withdrawal of Hungarian Honved troops from the front. All these symptoms, of course, were sharply observed by the Germans and also naturally by the population of the country itself. These diverging opinions and attitudes created a rather tense situation in the country.

In the first days of April of the year 1943, Kallay travelled to Rome to visit Mussolini and to pay a visit to Pope Pius XII. It did not remain a secret that Kallay brought up his plans for peace at both places and received friendly and understanding statements but complete refusals.

A few days later Hitler invited the Regent to the Castle of Klessheim near the city of Salzburg. In spite of the rather brief comments of the press, we obtained a lot of confidential information of this rather secret meeting. Competent official circles saw to it that the public were informed; the reason and aim of such disclosures were quite obvious. The invitation aimed at the clarification of military questions. As usual the Fuhrer started the negotiations with a torrent of complaints directed against the Regent; that the Honved Army was not fighting enough and this was the cause of his failures on the Eastern front; that the Rumanians were much better soldiers; that they were conducting a double-barreled policy; and he finally demanded new Honved units be sent to the fronts against the Soviets. The Regent proud of his position, his historical background, and his name, unlike Kalman Daranyi, did not remain cold and reserved against these rude remarks; instead, he refuted the accusations of Hitler rather forcefully and emphasized that the Germans did not keep their promises. Furthermore, he refused to send new troops to the front; on the contrary, he demanded that the Honved units be withdrawn from the first lines and sent back to their own country. He reasoned that this was necessary because of the hostile attitudes of our neighbors. Horthy also demanded that the Hungarian food shipments be paid for by the Third Reich in Pengo, the Hungarian monetary unit. He acceded to only one wish, namely, that the drafting of the Hungarian Schwabs into German units be continued. The official communique pertaining to these negotiations was changed many times and consisted only of a very brief statement that Budapest and Berlin were continuing their unshaken battle against the Communists. Horthy, after his return, sent a letter to Hitler in which he again refuted all accusations and emphasized further Hungary's loyal attitude toward her German ally. Kallay, at the same time, in a letter to Mussolini asked him to kindly interfere and explain in a benevolent manner his intentions to Hitler. Apparently Mussolini acceded to the wishes of Kallay but with little results, for the Hungarian Prime Minister was observed from Germany with the same unchanged mistrust. They had good reason to do so, however, Kallay delivered, in the month of May, a speech in which he stated that he was going to introduce a reserved policy towards the Third Reich. At the same time, as a gesture toward the Western allies, he emphasized that Hungary had never had the intention of acquiring new territorial rights through force of arms but desired only those areas which were detached from her, that Hungary did not want to change her constitution, and that he did not intend to introduce any further measures against the Jews. I have to mention here that this speech was not favourably received in Hungary. First, it seemed rather risky to make such statements against the Third Reich when it was known that she would react with all her aggressive force. Second, it was considered valueless to make such expiating statements toward the English and the Americans. As a result of the speech, left wing elements became loud and rather shady and long-forgotten political personalities emerged again.

At the end of July 1943, the Italian King removed Mussolini. This news spread like brush fire in Hungary and created great surprise. The question was whether the Italians were going to conclude a separate peace treaty and even eventually declare war on the Third Reich. I was able to make the following evaluation of the waves of our inner political life. The Marxists factions manifested in many ways their hope for the future. My friend Endre Bajcsi-Zsilinszky together with Zoltan Tildy, the president of the Small Holders Party, handed over a rather extensive memorandum to Kallay in which they made proposals for the future development of political trends. The right wing parties rattled their sabres on the side of the Germans and in the interest of the continuation of the war. The Government Party divided into groups and they debated their opposing opinions in lengthy conferences. The military circles emphasized that they were going to follow the orders of the Regent in all loyalty, but at the present moment would consider any decisive step as very risky and futile. Similar opinions were developed by those personalities who thought that the future policies of the country should follow the actions of the Anglo-Saxon powers in Italy and their successes in the Balkans.

Everybody was, of course, convinced that Kallay was going to increase his activities towards London and Washington. Very little was known about the details, however, and the public did not pay too much attention to them. Many started to listen, however, to the communications of the BBC radio, according to which the English air force was going to bombard Budapest if the Hungarian industry did not cease to produce for the German Wehrmacht. It was also known that the Czechs and the Rumanians had in London personalities in exile to whom the British Government was lending an ear. It was also observed that in Rumania, Croatia, and even in Slovakia, the anti-Hungarian attitude was spreading in spite of the fact that the Kallay government did not spare friendly gestures towards them. For instance, Kallay sent Count Miklos Banffy, former Minister of Foreign Affairs and rather popular Transylvanian land owner, to negotiate with the Rumanians.

In August the country learned that Miklos Kallay did not intend to change anything in the flow of the affairs. He expressed this standpoint to only a few of the leading personalities of the opposition parties. His position did not remain a secret, of course, but at the same time served to create a certain stability of opinion.

The opposition, among them also the Marxists, bowed to him because they were afraid of an eventual occupation of the country by the Germans. The right wing parties acknowledged the statement that he wanted to continue the war on the side of he Germans with satisfaction. Those elements who, with great scrutiny, put everything on the scale obtained reassurance that the government was not going to undertake any adventures which would result in an immediate and merciless German takeover. Had that occured, we could not have counted on any effective help from the Anglo-Saxon powers.

In the meantime, the allies landed in Sicily and continued their thrust towards Rome. The Italian Army, in compliance with the stipulations of the armistice which General Badoglio had concluded with the Anglo-Saxons, put down their arms and the German army units, fighting in Italy, withdrew towards the north. The German Government demanded that the Hungarian Government arrest every Italian civilian or member of a military organization or individual in the country and that all shipments directed to Italy be immediately cancelled and stopped. The Regent summoned all outstanding and leading personalities of the country to a conference at which they decided to refuse all German demands and ordered that a military mission be sent to Berlin to negotiate the withdrawal of the Hungarian army units fighting on the eastern front. If the Germans did not accede to this request of the government, the Regent, using his power as supreme commander of the army, was going to order their return. All the general public knew about this conference was that the policy of the government was going to be drawn in accordance with the interest of the country. At the end of September, a military mission headed by the Chief of Staff, General Szombathelyi, traveled to Hitler, who immediately and categorically declined the withdrawal of Hungarian Honved units from the eastern front. He demanded that they should be sent to the Balkans and utilized for tactical moves introduced to halt the allied forces. This demand was refused by Szombathelyi. Finally, the military decided that only to a certain extent and only certain lines of the Hungarian railroads were to be used for transportation of the German Army and its supplies and that the Germans were not going to insist on the increase of food supply shipments.

In October German Admiral Raeder came to Budapest and reported to the Regent that Hitler was presenting him with a luxuryyacht. This rather tactless gift created great resentment and painful surprise all over the country. Since Hungary did not have any sea, it is easy to see why such a present was rather misplaced: more so, since Admiral Raeder delivered an outstanding lecture in front of a selected and large audience in the Houses of Parliament, in the course of which he stated that the German fleet would not be able to defend the Adriatic Sea. As far as I know, Raeder did not negotiate about any military or political questions.

Also in October the two Houses of the Parliament convened to deal with the budget of the country. The uneasiness of the public was mirrored in the speeches made in the course of the debates. Count Janos Zichy and Count Antal Sigray, both of the opposition party, propagated a Christian Democratic program and demanded that the war be ended immediately on our side and that we detach ourselves from the Third Reich. Against all this, the Right Wing representatives made loud speeches in the interest of the efficient continuation of the war. Bela Imredy, who was so very much reserved towards the Germans before, emphasized loyalty to the Third Reich and accused the Hungarian Government of a double-faced policy. From these statements a very heated debate developed between him and Kallay. The members of the Small Holders Party talked about the spreading of Bolshevism, whereas the Social Democrats openly requested an Anglo-Saxon orientation and protested against dictatorial methods.

The attitude of the Hungarian press also reflected all the characteristic trends of the rather perplexed public. The Marxist papers came out with articles which the courts could have easily prosecuted as treacherous at any time. Milotay, congressional representative and noted publicist, wrote articles about the victory of the Germans and stated that the allies could not gain victory in Europe. Representative Jaross wrote in one of his articles that the Bolshevist imperialism could be smashed only by the Germans. The paper entitled **Hungary** printed articles asking that since there was no enemy at her frontiers as yet, to whom should Hungary lay down her arms? The Government press could hardly find any explanation for the very precarious situation of the country.

In November a very good friend of mine, Representative Bela Jurcsek, visited Berlin. He was an expert in public alimentation and worked out an excellent plan for the improvement of the food distribution which was deteriorating more and more. His plan was accepted by the Government and entrusted to him for execution. Jurcsek traveled to Germany in this capacity to negotiate a possible decrease of food shipments. Upon his return, he related to me how unpopular Kallay was in the Third Reich and he also mentioned, and I quote: "Hungary is full of German spies."

At the end of the year, the Hungarian Government renewed its investigations of the terror actions committed in 1941 in the course of the occupation of the Bacska. These investigations were interrupted upon the request of the Germans and the military in those times. As a consequence of the investigations, two generals, General Cejder and General Grassi, and some other officers were sentenced to prison. In accordance with the Hungarian Military Penal Code, high ranking officers may be freed upon their own recognizance. The two generals and also two staff officers were granted this privilege, upon which they immediately escaped to Germany and were accepted into the SS formations at their old Hungarian rank. This news created extremely great resentment in Hungary, not only because Hungarian Honved officers broke their word of honor, but mainly because of the fact that a so-called ally immediately engaged their services in her armed forces. It should be emphasized, however, that all four of the above officers were of German extraction.

Also at the end of the year, several new civilian organizations were created, such as: the "Turani Vadaszok" (Translated: Turanian Hunters), "Szekely Loveszek" (Translated: Sekler Fusiliers), and the "Nemzet Vedelmi Kereszt" (Translated: National Defence Cross). All of these organizations aimed to improve security conditions by serving loyally the person of the Regent and eventually fighting against subversive elements and the communists by force of arms if necessary. All three organizations had members of all walks of Hungarian life and the number was placed around four hundred—five hundred thousand. I, myself, belonged to the National Defense Cross organization. I studied its aims and evaluated its importance. The organization was comprised exclusively of patriotic elements who were against subversion even in 1918 during the communist terror regime of Bela Kun. The Cross emblem was donated to them by the Regent. Sometime later a young lawyer Karoly Ney, under the influence of Imredy, organized another

56

association called "Keleti Arcvonal Bajtarsi Szovetseg" (Translated: Eastern Front Collegiate Federation). Much later in the year 1945, Ney formed a battalion of a few hundred young boys who fought valiantly against the occupying Soviet forces.

At the beginning of the tragic year 1944, influenced by the news of the nearing of the Russian Army, the political and press circles and the majority of the country requested and demanded that the country's defense be bolstered. We hoped that the mountain chain of the Carpathians would stop the Red Army. This was the opinion of the Endre Bajcsi-Zsilinsky and his adherents; the same characterizing the Christian Democrats, the party of Imredy, and that of the Government (MEP). Opinion diverged only on one point: whether this defense should be developed with the help of the Germans, with the help of the allies, or should be done alone with our own armed forces through an entire mobilization of the country. With the exception of the Marxists, public opinion was leaning toward the decision to fight on the side of the Germans because this was the only way to keep the Russians from overrunning the country. It was felt, however, that food shipments and industrial supplies to the Third Reich should be decreased. The political leadership of Kallay followed the requirements of this developing public opinion and, being aware of the intimate and friendly relationship between the Regent and Kallay, no one doubted that this attitude and trend was condoned and approved by Horthy and the Honved Army. The confidence of the country in the force of her arms was so great that even the ever opposing Count Istvan Bethlen, former Minister President and Lower House Representative, proposed at one of the sessions of the defence committee of the Lower House that the Honveds occupy those parts of Transylvania which were left to the Rumanians and take defense positions in the southern Carpathians in the snowy mountain chains of Szoreny and Vulkan. His speech was received with great acclamation, although everybody knew that such action against Rumania would not be possible without the approval of the Germans and that the Rumanian Army, which was in readiness against Soviet Russians, obviously would have turned against us and war would have broken out.

At the beginning of the year 1944, preparations were started for a general mobilization. Fortifications were constructed in the Carpatho-Ruthenian and Hungarian-Transylvanian sectors of the Carpathian mountain chains. The supply shipments of food staples to the Third Reich were noticeably reduced. The Government Party (MEP) voted confidence to Kallay. Futhermore, everyone was convinced that he was continuing his secret diplomatic activities with the Anglo-Saxon allies. When news was spread about the internment of some English officers at the castle of Count Mihaly Andrassy at Szigetvar, however, the question was put up whether they were really prisoners of war or secret political agents preparing the take over of Trans-danubia by parachutists.

Although the press was completely silent, it was well known that our Chief of Staff General Szombathelyi paid a visit in January to Hitler and to Keitel. It was felt that, while there, Szombathelyi probably negotiated about the return of the Honved Army units to the country and about the defense of the Hungarian Carpathian Line. We also heard vague news which stated that the Germans declined the release of the Hungarian Army but at the same time promised to send adequate forces to defend Hungary. (This was something we were afraid of.)

Well, I remember how feverishly the population of the country was preparing for the national holiday of March 15. This was to be a great demonstration in the interest of a free and independent Hungary with a strong army and with a social and economic life based on the ideas of Szeged: vanquishing the Communist threat and regaining the old historical position in the Valley of the Danube.

But then came the fatal 19th of March of the year 1944.

Before I start with the description of the political consequences of this tragic day, I would like to say a few words about the actions of the Hungarian Expeditionary Force sent to the front. In this brief description I have used the outstanding and factual book of Vitez Ferenc Adonyi, former major in the General Staff, entitled "The Hungarian Soldier in the Second World War."

I stated previously that the Hungarian Government turned over to the disposition of the Wehrmacht the so-called Second Hungarian Army, composed of the III, IV, VII Honved Army Corps. This Hungarian Expeditionary Army moved on to the Soviet Russian front between April and July in the year 1942.

In these months the military situation was as follows: in compliance with the strategic plans of Hitler, German General Weichs received orders to move with his army groups (Armee Gruppe B) attacking towards Voronyezs. This was done for the protection of the left wing of the German main forces thrusting forward towards the region of the Caucasian Mountains and Stalingrad. General Weichs started his tactical moves in June of the year 1942 from the Kurks-Bjelograd-Wolcsansk triangle. The Third Hungarian Army Corps, a part of the Second Hungarian Army, arrived at the front first and immediately participated in the tactical moves of the Weichs Army Group by cutting through the Russian lines and in the beginning of July they reached the River Don. Here the Third Corps was joined by the Fourth and Seventh Corps of the Honved Army which became also attached to the Weichs Army Group. Half way through the year 1944, while battle was carried on for Stalingrad, the Second Hungarian Army held a front approximately 200 kilometers long along the River Don: the approximate geographical location being near the cities of Voronyezs-Urym-Csucsje.

At that time Hugo Stinnes was again in Budapest. We had dinner together in one of the well-known restaurants of Buda and since I knew that he had two sons fighting at Stalingrad, I asked him what news he had of them. He became very serious and after a period of painful silence, he said the following and I quote: "Listen, Mr. Baross. The end will be a 'Festung Mittleuropa' (Translated: Middle European fortress) and it is questionable whether we will be able to hold it." I asked him with great concern: "But, for heaven's sake, what is going to happen to Hungary then?" Upon which he answered: "Hungary is going to be either inside the fortress or outside, but she is going to be annihilated in any case." The writer remarks here that Stinnes hinted to the eventuality that Hungary may detach herself from the Third Reich. We finished our dinner in prolonged silence and I, after a sleepless night, hurried up to the Fortress to see Miklos Kallay and to tell him what Stinnes had said. Listening to my words, his face became darker and darker and then suddenly a broad smile appeared and he said: "Tell your friends that as long as I am sitting here, in this position, we are going to stick to the Germans." His answer, knowing his political activities, greatly surprised me.

Neither the Honved Army nor the German Wehrmacht fighting on her left wing nor the Italians on her right wing were able to cross the River Don, nor were they able to stop Soviet Russians in order to build beach heads on the right river bank. The German Armies fought futile battles with great losses in the Stalingrad region. The situation deteriorated day by day at the Don front and the Germans sent spare units from their whole army and directed them to go to Stalingrad. The remaining scattered army fractions were without necessary reserves and adequate equipment to fight the unusually severe winter conditions any farther. Having fought many, many battles without cessation, they were slowly becoming inadequate to face an eventual aggressive thrust of the Soviet Russian Army.

The expected Soviet Russian attack came in January 1943 on the Don front and, in spite of heroic resistance and fighting, they mowed down all resistance. The Third Hungarian Army Corps, after great sacrifices in side and rear protective actions, fell into captivity. The Fourth and Seventh Army Corps, having been filled up with the occupation army units and a cavalry corps, built up a defense line in the Valley of the River Oskol. There, the remnants of the German Army concentrated in the region of Charkov and prepared for a counterattack. The months to follow presented ups and downs in the chances of battle. Soon the Italian Army was withdrawn from the front. The Hungarian Army and her remaining battle groups were united in the so-called First Honved Army.

It was in July that the fighting armies heard about the downfall of Mussolini, the formation of the Government of Italian General Badoglio, the laying down of arms by the Italians, and the landing of the Anglo-Saxon powers on Sicily. It was also about that time that our Chief of Staff General Szombathelyi reported and I quote: "The occupation of the vast territories and the overpowering numbers of the enemy make it impossible for the Germans to deliver a decisive blow to any of their adversaries. The continuation of strategic moves may be only aiming to gain time and postpone decisive action." The Hungarian General Staff also reported the observation that the Germans were concentrating troops along the Hungarian border, in particular in the Burgenland. This was noteworthy because Hungary was the only so-called "Allied State" where there were no German army units garrisoned. This observation was reported to the Government by the General Staff.

At the beginning of the year 1944, the Soviet Russians launched an aggressive and immense attack from the direction of Krivograd-Tserkasky-Krivojrog and the Crimea. The Ukraine was soon given up and the entire front withdrew into the foreground of the Carpathian Mountains. The defense positions were taken north of Lemberg by the German Heeresgruppe Mitte (Translated: Middle Army Group). From Lemberg stretching to Stanislaw stood the First Hungarian Army and south from it the Heeresgruppe Sud-Ukraine, (Translated: South Ukrainian Army Group) consisting of German and Rumanian Army units. The First Hungarian Army was reinforced. In the Carpathians, from the Dukla Pass down to the Szekely Snow Mountain Chains, fortifications were constructed. Thus was the military situation on March 19 of the year 1944.

At the start of March, several friends and I decided to spend a few weeks in the resort area of Borszek, which is located in the snowy mountain chain of Gyergyo. We left the capital city of Budapest in the atmosphere of preparation for a grandiose celebration of the national holiday of March 15. We spent carefree days in the beautiful pine forest of Borszek. What could have been the cause of our cheerful mood? Maybe the fact that the Anglo-Saxon powers had landed in Italy and that their advance was very rapid. Perhaps because we had placed our confidence in the attack which the Allies had launched on the Balkan Peninsula, or were hopeful that the regroupment of the armies fighting on the eastern front would result in favorable developments. Today, if I look back to those beautiful days, all this seems to be incomprehensible. We heard through newspaper articles that Hitler had sent the Regent a renewed invitation for a personal visit. The Regent traveled on March 17 to meet "the Fuhrer" in Klessheim. We had great hopes, also, as to the outcome of these negotiations because we thought that the Regent would be able to persuade Hitler to let the Hungarian Armies that were fighting in the East return to their proper country in order to defend it.

60

In the early morning hours of March 19, my very good friend Representative Kalman Konkoly-Thege, who was together with us at Borszek, woke me up with the words "there must have been something terrible happening at Budapest." He also stated that it was impossible to obtain any news through the telephone. We made several attempts during the day to make connections with Budapest or with Kolozsvar. The telephone switchboards always answered with the stereotyped phrase: "Lines are busy." In the evening of the same day, the station master of the railroad station of Borszek, located in the town of Marosheviz, telephoned the managers of our hotel and communicated to them that the last train to Budapest would depart the next day, March 20, at six o'clock in the morning. He also suggested that any guests who wanted to return to the capital should prepare for their departure. Upon the surprised attitude and questions of the hotel director, the station master answered only by saying, "The Germans are in the country."

We all departed. At every important railroad station German military police were present. At the eastern station of Budapest we could see that all the installations were occupied by German soldiers.

What happened? Numerous German army units had entered into Hungary on foot, on motor vehicles, armored cars, tanks and airplanes coming from Rumania, Yugoslavia, Austria, and Slovakia. In general, the negligible Honved forces had let them through and at only a few places did skirmishes develop and these resulted in a few dead and wounded. The Wehrmacht and SS units swiftly occupied all important railroad and highway junctions, bridges, tunnels, and everything that could be considered tactically important. In Budapest the Gestapo set up their headquarters in the Hotel Astoria. When the Regent returned from Klessheim in the morning of March 19, the occupation of Hungary had already been completed. He was received at the Kelenfold Station by the three star German General Weichs and a German honor company. The members of the Cabinet and Kallay were also present. The population of Budapest saw only that much and knew only these events. Did the foregoing actions of the Germans invite the ire of the nation or did they merely surprise people? It could hardly be known for certain. The masses in the capital city and in the nation thought that all this had happened with the approval of the Hungarian Government, and that these measures were necessary and in the interest of an efficient defense by the country against the threatening proximity of the Soviet Russian Army.

But what had really happened? Political circles learned pretty soon that the Regent had traveled to Klessheim accompanied by the Chief of General Staff General Szombathelyi, Deputy Foreign Minister Ghiczy, and Defense Minister Csatay. There in a private conversation between Hitler and the Regent, the details of which were told to me at a later date, Hitler communicated that because the Hungarian political attitudes were in dire contradiction to the German interests, he had decided on and had ordered the occupation of Hungary. The Regent vehemently opposed all Hitler's accusations and he threatened Hitler with armed resistance. Similar was the tone of the negotiations conducted between Szombathelyi and Keitel, and between Ghiczy and Ribbentrop. The Hungarians were forced to drop the idea of armed resistance quite soon because of the fact that Hungary's combatant troops were fighting the Soviet Russians on the eastern front and that they could not have been withdrawn easily from there. Also the Honved units had not completed their mobilization in Hungary proper and thus, because they were only scantily armed, their resistance would have been very ineffectual. In the negotiations Hungary agreed to speed up the mobilization of the Army, to send new Honved units to the front, to turn over the use of the Hungarian railroad lines to the disposition of the German Army, and to increase the industrial production in order to supply the Germans with needed equipment; but all these agreements were made under the condition that in turn the Germans would regard the occupation of the country as temporary and would eventually withdraw all their armies, leaving not more than two or three divisions. Political circles, which had access to more confidential information, were under the impression that Hitler had probably also demanded from the Regent a more radical solution of the Jewish problem and also requested the immediate removal of Kallay; meanwhile making faint promises about the continuation of the Hungarian rule and supremacy. The press was silent about all these dark things and, if I am not mistaken, there were no press communiques of the Klessheim visit: all that was stated was that it had happened. Some newspapers abroad gave more or less detailed accounts about the occupation of Hungary.

After his arrival in Budapest, the Regent summoned the Crown Council, the members of the Government, and some other important personalities. Some well-informed persons maintain that the Regent relieved Kallay and his Government of their duties at this Crown Council; however, others state that the Government abdicated. A new Government had not yet been designated at that time.

The next day the Gestapo started its activities; it arrested hundreds of people, among them members of Parliament, and held them in custody in the cellars of the Hotel Astoria.

On March 22, as planned much earlier, the Houses of Parliament opened their sessions; but after the few opening words by the President of the Lower House Andras Tasnadi-Nagy, a motion was made to adjourn for an indefinite time, and this motion was accepted immediately without a single opposing comment from the entire House.

The new Government headed by Sztojai was sworn into office

on March 23. The Cabinet consisted of four members of the Government Party (MEP), three members of the Imredy party, two generals and the right wing of National Socialist Party, which was represented in the Ministry of the Interior through the appointment of Under Secretary Baky. The task of this Government was to unify all the national forces serving the nation and bring them into close, friendly relationship with the Germans. This fact was emphasized in a statement published in the official gazette about the formation of the new Government, in which they also hinted to the fact that the German Army units had "arrived" in agreement with the Hungarian Government.

There are many official and unofficial statements in circulation about the formation of this Government. Of these statements, the following are considered by the author as authentic. After the negotiations conducted at Klessheim, Hitler nominated Dr. Edmund Veesenmayer to be Ambassador and Minister Plenipotentiary to Budapest with the task to bring the Hungarian Government policies in unison with the interests of the Third Reich. Veesenmayer was a Himmler man and there is trustworthy information that he had traveled to Hungary several times under an alias in order to study the general situation and Kallay's political activities. Veesenmayer arrived in Budapest on the same train as the Regent and replaced Jagow as German Ambassador; he immediately sought connections with various Hungarian political circles and even found his way to the Regent. Political activities were also developed under another German official SS staff officer Kaltenbrunner, who was commanding the SS troops which were occupying Hungary. Both Veesenmayer and Kaltenbrunner tried to influence the selection and formation of the new Government. Veesenmayer proposed that Imredy be the Minister President, but this was rigidly declined by the Regent. After that, Veesenmayer left the selection of the ministers to the Regent in order "to preserve the aspects of constitutional basis" and instead proposed that the Regent form a coalition government of right wing elements.

The Regent selected Sztojai because in Berlin he was a "Persona Grata," besides being a soldier whose loyal intentions he did not doubt. I knew all the members of the new Cabinet with the exception of Sztojai and Csatay. In those times I had very close relationships with many old timers in politics and with numerous members of the Houses of Parliament. Therefore, it is easy for me to reconstruct the happenings on the basis of the talks that I had with them.

It remained unclear and subject to discussion whether the Kallay Government knew of the plans of the Germans to occupy Hungary, and if so, why they did not undertake any action to hinder them. All important friends of mine were of the opinion that Kallay knew about the German intentions against Hungary, or at least suspected them. It has been noted above that our general staff submitted reports to the Government about the German troop concentrations along the Hungarian border, and the staff also reported observations about Rumanian, Yugoslavian, Croatian, and Slovak Army movements. The Government definitely knew about the intrigues conducted by the Rumanians in Berlin and also was aware of the news which reached Hungary from abroad pertaining to the German intentions. But why were no measures undertaken? From many sources I heard that Kallay did not believe that the Germans would dare use force against Hungary. Notably, force would not be used because it would have immediately invited the resistance of the entire Hungarian public opinion, and created armed resistance in the back of the German supply lines; many were also of the opinion that Kallay also considered the possibility that to have a German occupation of Hungary would be clear testimony before the Allies of Hungary's attitude and would have improved her situation and future possibilities. Thus, he firmly believed that the Third Reich was not going to take this risk. The military command of Hungary further stated that an armed resistance would be impossible because the combat-ready Honved Army units were fighting against the Soviet Russian armies in the east, and since they were far away from the mother country, their return would have been impossible without having been disarmed by the Germans. On the other hand, the units stationed in the country were not completely ready and did not possess modern arms either.

Soon after the Sztojai Government entered office, the "co-ordinated" political methods became obvious. Minister of the Interior Jaross undertook measures to herd all Jews together, to intern them and to ship them to Germany. The prisoners of the Gestapo numbered several thousands already. Among them were Cabinet ministers, generals, diplomats, and Anglophile aristocrats, and such personalities who came there because of denunciations. Former Minister President Kallay himself escaped arrest by taking refuge in the Turkish Embassy. These political prisoners were kept in the cellar of the Hotel Astoria, from there they were shipped to German concentration camps. The Honved army divisions were mobilized one after the other in a great hurry, and a Fortification Command was established to construct different lines in the Carpathian Mountains. It is true that the number of German Army units stationed in Hungary was reduced, but some tactically important points in the country were furnished with German command positions like, for instance, the Bacska, Carpatho-Ruthenia, and Transylvania. These German Army commands had to preserve a good relationship, so-called Hungarian "liaison commissioners" attached to them. Besides the German Army, there were many secret German organizations in the country. They all were studded with spies and denunciators. Their chief was a certain Winkelmann, also a Himmler, and a former police officer who had his headquarters in the confiscated English Embassy building; innumerable Hungarians became involved with these terrible figures of history who had a decisive influence in the formation of Hungarian fate.

The Anglo-Saxon air raids started in April. Besides the great and important industrial plants of military and civilian value, they also bombed the city of Budapest and other open cities, thereby causing great damages in life and material.

What was the attitude of the country itself as it observed all these happenings? According to my own observations, the villages, country towns, and even the population of Budapest itself witnessed these events with a sort of inertia. Their attentions were attracted more to the happenings of the eastern front and to the difficulties of public maintenance of nutrition. Different, however, were the trends in the political scene. There, there were innumerable opinions, contradictory evaluations, personal controversies; and the new groups split and fragmented the important and influential circles. Because the Houses of Parliament were indefinitely adjourned, there was no forum for exchange and clarification of ideas; a place where possibly relationships could have been reestablished. The Sztojai Government had neither prestige nor influence. The press, acceding to the pressure of personalities and political trends, lost its authoritativeness. In a few month, the well-balanced Hungarian political scene lost its fine atmosphere and instead presented the picture of anarchy. All this facilitated the strong organization of secret Marxist-Leninist elements in spite of the vigilance of the German and Hungarian police.   ,

In June, I reported for active duty in the army. They called me and I was detailed to the Hungarian Fortification Command located in Budapest. This command had the task of constructing defense positions in the Carpathian Mountains. Before I reported to my position in the army, I requested an audience from the Regent. I intended to give him a report about my observations pertaining to the political situation in the country. He had previously received me many, many times in similar questions and aspects. In the course of the audience, after having made my report on my observations, he thanked me and then, in accordance with his usual phraseology, he said the following and I quote: "... Now listen here, Baross ... ," and then without any further ado, with always increasing vehemence, jumping up from his seat and pacing up and down in the room, he started to complain about the meeting at Klessheim. He told me in detail about Hitler's shouting and his obscene remarks, and I quote, "... He is going to send the Slovaks, the Rumanians, and the Serbs, against me ... ," and also of Hitler's absolutely overpowering attitude against the Regent's person and against that of his entourage, and I quote, "... They kept me literally a prisoner ... ;" and then went on to tell me Hitler's denial of the return of the Honved Army units to Hungary, and of Hitler's great hatred for Kallay and others, and his dejecting opinions about the Hungarian soldiers. My audience lasted one hour and fifteen minutes, and I took leave greatly disturbed and deeply moved. I was joined in the antechamber by General Karoly Lazar, the commander of the Royal Body Guard, and we left the Royal Palace together. He noted my exhausted condition and asked me, and I quote, "What happened?" And I told him that "... he complained about the attitude of the Germans." Upon which Lazar answered, "One cannot complain enough." And then we took leave without any further words from each other.

I will now give some details about the happenings on the front as they were known to me and also based upon the writings of Colonel Adonyi.

I already mentioned above that in March, the front was pushed back to the foothills of the Carpathian Mountains. The command of the First Hungarian Army was taken over by General Naday. In the meantime, the army was reinforced with new divisions brought into battle readiness and was detailed to the "Heeresgruppe Nord-Ukraine" under the command of General Mannstein, and later under that of General Model. The task of this army was to conduct an attack towards the Dnyester River, and in the course of this move General Naday proposed that the Hungarian units be placed in defense positions on the eastern slopes of the Carpathians. The "Heeresgruppe" attacks saw a few beginning successes, then came to a stop against the outnumbering Soviet Russian forces, and then they formed a rigid line along Kuty-Delatyn-Ottinia-Stanislaw. The First Hungarian Army received new reinforcements from the home country in this position, and its divisions were dispersed among other Wehrmacht divisions. Parallel with the landing of the Anglo-Saxon Armies in Normandy, the Russian Soviet Armies launched a major attack in June against this defense line aiming to thrust through this line and take the Polish oil fields defended by the Heeresgruppe Mitte. As a result of this major attack, the German divisions were drawn away from the foothills of the Carpathian Mountains and sent to the fronts which were in immediate danger, and the Hungarian divisions were again united into the First Hungarian Army. The Soviet Russian attack developed during July along the front held by the First Hungarian Army.

This was the month when the Fortification Command and its headquarters were transferred from Budapest to the town of Beregszasz, located in Carpatho-Ruthenia. From there the Command was better able to supervise and to lead the fortification procedures and construction of the defense lines. As a member of his staff, I was able to observe the progress of these defense constructions. In the Carpatho-Ruthenian sector the concrete fortification systems were ready and they would have been able to hold against all types of attacks. But in the Transylvanian sector of the Hungarian frontier, they were in the beginning stages, and the technical engineer battalions assigned to this duty were trying to advance the state of these by working day and night on the project. Also in the course of our inspection tours I was able to observe partisan activities in the northern sectors of the virgin forest of the Carpathians. In this region everybody was fighting everybody. The Poles fought the Ukrainians, and both of them killed Germans. But, with us Hungarians, there was some kind of a secret sympathy and the partisans manifested their friendly feelings toward us in multifarious ways. Nevertheless, it was very, very dangerous to drive along the valleys of the Carpathian Mountains in a vehicle. I myself was also subject to several machine bursts, and in order to avoid such misunderstandings, we equipped our motor vehicles with huge red, white, and green flags. The Soviet attack progressed slowly on the fronts held by the First Hungarian Army, but their immensely larger numbers finally pushed and forced the heroically fighting Honved back into the Hunyadi fortification lines constructed in the northern and eastern Carpathians. These tactical moves were directed by three star General Beregfi, who had replaced General Lakatos when he was called back to Budapest. Beregfi was of German origin and was a National Socialist with regard to his political opinions. He was rather negligent in sending reinforcements to the Carpathian Mountains; and therefore, the Hugarian Army Command substituted him quite soon with three star General Miklos, who established his headquarters at Huszt in Carpatho-Ruthenia. He immediately moved three Honved divisions to defense positions on the passes of Verecke and Uzsok.

August 23 was a very memorable day, for at the headquarters of the Fortification Command at Beregszasz we received a very surprising telephone call which reported that some Rumanian troops had come up to the Hungarian border under white flags, had requested passage through the mountain pass and had been granted such because our control point had considered them soldiers who belonged to some mixed German and Rumanian units in retreat. Such occurrences were very frequent along the Hungarian-Rumanian border. Thus, these Rumanians reached the next village without being disturbed and started to kill the civilian population. The engineer battalion, which was on defense constructions of the Bekas pass, immediately went into action against them and annihilated them. In the noon hours of the same day we learned that the entire Rumanian Army had deserted and had gone over to the Russians: The Rumanian Army who had been the pet child of the Third Reich and whose loyalty Hitler never doubted. They immediately attacked the rear of the "Heeresgruppe Sud-Ukraine" under the command of German three star General Friessner.

This treachery of the Rumanians opened the road through

Rumania to Southern Transylvania for the Soviet Russian Armies of Marshal Malinowsky. At the same time Marshal Tolbuchin occupied Bulgaria. The First Hungarian Army defended all sectors of the northern and eastern Carpathians with rigid and undiminishing resistance under the renewed and constant attacks by the Russians. At the same time a Second Hungarian Army which had been formed under the command of General Lajos Veress and reinforced by several German units was trying to stop the onslaught of the Soviet Russian and Rumanian forces attacking the southern Carpathian chain along the Maros River. At this time the Germans disarmed the other outstanding "pride" of the Third Reich, the two Slovak divisions, before they were able to desert and put down their arms in front of their Slavic brothers.

The Fortification Command and its headquarters were transferred in the first days of September from Beregszasz to Budapest, and I was transferred with a few officers to the railroad junction of Csap to organize the shipment of the technical materials to the fortification works in the interior of the country. After Russian bombers raided and severely damaged Csap on September 17, I received orders to move into Budapest.

During September and October, the Second and Third Honved Armies, the latter having been organized in the meantime under the command of General Heszlenyi, fought major battles along the River Maros, and at the cities of Kolozsvar, Nagyvarad, Debrecen, and Arad. The Soviet Russian Army, outnumbering all resistance, was pushing back the Armee Gruppe-Sud under the command of three star General Friessner. This "Armee-Gruppe" retreated towards the River Tisza as it was pushed back by Malinowsky's armies and by Tolbuchin's units which were pressing in from Bulgaria. The First Hungarian Army, defending firmly the Carpathian frontier line — to avoid an eventual attack from the rear — bent its strategic lines down towards the Tisza River. In the middle of October, the Soviet Russians more or less reached the line of Baja-Kecskemet-Szolnok-Tokaj-Eperjes.

On Sunday, October 15, 1944, while walking from my home at about 10 a.m. to attend Holy Mass to meet with a few fellow officers in the church located at the Esku Place, I observed that there were Honved patrols walking up and down the streets with bayonets mounted. At the Esku Place I saw a platoon manning machine guns. There, there was a crowd of the civilian population also gazing at the happenings. I found my fellow officers after great difficulty ond one of them, who lived at the Esku Place, related the following. Miklos Horthy Jr., the son of the Regent, had been arrested by the Germans in the offices of the Magyar Folyam es Tengerhajozasi Tarsasag [Translated into English: Hungarian River and Sea Faring Association]. There he was knocked out, wrapped in a blanket and hurried away in a vehicle, upon which the garrison of Budapest was placed on the alert and around the Esku Place military patrols took over. We decided to return to our homes because of the obvious alert, and to wait there for further orders which would eventually be issued by the Fortification Command. At noon on the same day I heard over the radio the statement of the Regent concerning the armistice. I listened, greatly moved, and very bitter thoughts came over about the future of Hungary. In the early afternoon hours I received a phone call from the Fortification Command to go immediately to the headquarters. There, Colonel Harosi of the Engineer Corps delivered a speech to the officers, non-commissioned officers and personnel and stated that the armistice did not mean that the war was over, but that we had to fight still and everybody ought to comply with his military duties. We had to prepare for the event that the mob was going eventually to take over the rule of Budapest and was eventually going to attack the military installations. Thus, also the Fortification Command, which had its custody and possession some very important documents, was going to defend these by force of arms if necessary. His words were received with general approval and consent and everybody thought that to comply with them was a national duty.

On October 16, the news reached us that the Regent had retracted his orders about the armistice and had abdicated. Colonel Harosi was arrested and he was replaced temporarily by a young member of the general staff, Captain Bencsik. Nobody was excited and everybody worked with great zeal on the tasks to be carried out.

On November 6, General Ulaszlo Solymossy took over the command. On November 10, the headquarters were transferred to the village of Ajka, located in the Bakony Mountains. On November 21, I learned there that I was detailed to the German "Armee Pioneer Fuhrung" [Translated into English: Army Engineering Command] of the German Army as a liaison officer. I reported for duty on November 28 to Colonel Schiermeister, an elderly man who was in command at the village of Nezsa in the county of Nograd.

On December 6, while on an inspection tour in the region of the town of Vac, we learned that our headquarters at Nezsa had been attacked and destroyed by Soviet Russian tanks. Since we could no longer return there, with some personnel of the Command we retreated with all motor vehicles towards the city of Ipolysag. For us, this move meant the start of the eternal wanderings. On April 1, 1945, Easter Sunday, at four o'clock I stepped across the Hungarian-Austrian frontier with the German units, leaving Hungary and Hungarian villages in flames. This is the last terrible, heart-rending picture of my country which I will carry forever in my soul.

The Hungarian soldier did not know much about the political undercurrents and happenings of internal and foreign policy which concentrated around the fatal date of October 15, and he was not very much interested in them. The Hungarian soldier had fought with a deathly and terrible bitterness because he wanted to protect his country.

APPENDIX TO THE TREATISE ENTITLED "HUNGARY AND HITLER"

I wish to emphasize again that my study entitled "Hungary and Hitler" was written entirely and exclusively on the basis of my private sources of information, my own observations and experiences. Here and there I had to check dates, and for this I used reliable and pertinent works. Therefore, I am of the opinion that my present study should be regarded as an authentic, original source of scientific information for historians.

Still I am of the opinion that this study needs some further explanation and completion. Namely, I think that I have to give certain background information pertaining to the events surrounding October 15, 1944: events which preceded this date and followed it. I was not able to observe all of these events personally because of my military service. I want to write about those more or less secret diplomatic connections which were maintained by various Hungarian governments with the "Western Allies," that is to say, with the enemies of the "Axis Powers," and those negotiations which were used in the interest of the Hungarian nation. I would like to mention also the questions surrounding the activities of the governments, formed abroad and remaining in exile, and finally, I would like to give an account of those intentions and occurences which were planned by the Pan-Germanic movement and which began towards the end of the Thirties, and to give details about those plans, which Hitler wanted to carry out, involving the future of Hungary.

Data pertaining to these questions were gathered by me in emigration after 1945 from statements by fellow refugees and on the basis of works of scientific value written by Hungarian or foreign authors. This collection of data and information is of value to elucidate more details of the painful and terrible years which characterized the connection between Hungary and Hitler.

Chapter I

THE SITUATION BEFORE AND AFTER OCTOBER 1944

The Sztojai Government feverishly worked on the reorientation of Hungarian public life. The leading personalities of public offices in the government proper and in the municipal administration and also in the spheres of education, were substituted with individuals who were sympathetic towards the politics and interests of the Third Reich. Thus, for instance, the outstanding and very loyal Chief of the General Staff General Szombathelyi was replaced by General Janos Voros. All these personnel changes resulted in strifes, antagonisms and growing anarchy between the various political parties, the Government Party, the followers of Imredy, the National Socialists, and the Arrow Corps movement, which all had a great influence on the events as already mentioned in my study. Bardossy, and later Sztojai, tried to smooth out these controversies, but without success. On the other hand, the opposition, or left wing political factor, was cut out pretty quickly and thoroughly by the Gestapo. The latter's activities did not spare circles adhering to the Small Holders Party and the Christian Social Party either.

In accordance with the interests of the Third Reich, Minister of the Interior Jaross, with the cooperation of his Under Secretary of State Baky and Laszlo Endre, started to carry out measures to settle the Jewish question. Being under the influence of the notorious Eichmann, Jaross was instigated to have the Jews arrested, taken to concentration camps, and later shipped to Germany. In those times there were many rumors pertaining to an understanding between a high ranking SS Staff officer and wealthy Jewish families, which gave the latter the opportunity to leave the country with all their belongings.

In May, Bela Imredy was designated top Minister of Economics and he expedited shipments of victuals and industrial products to Germany.

The foreign political machinations soon became impossible because of the well-planned vigilance of the Germans. Nevertheless, they were continued and information pertaining to some actions reached me also. For instance, my very good friend Andras Hory, our former Ambassador to Warsaw, maintained a relationship and communication with former Minister President Mihajlovic, leader of the Yugoslav Royalists, and he even visited him. At the same time the Allies introduced widespread left wing propaganda in Hungary. Of course, the Soviet Russians immediately started a Communist underground movement. In London, Count Mihaly Karolyi started a "Free Hungary" movement. This movement was formed in London by former officers of the Ministry of Foreign Affairs and also diplomats who had become "dissidents," and this, of course, was a chance for doing good work in the interest of the country. It is said that Washington D.C. was under the false impression that the leftists were the only national democratic forces and that she did not keep in contact with the expatriot circles, but dealt exclusively with the leftist ones. The Allied Air Force conducted heavy air raids against the country and neither the Hungarian nor the German anti-aircraft batteries could stop these raids and as a result caused the Hungarians to lose their faith in the good will of the Anglo-Saxon powers.

This tense and rather mournful atmosphere was characterized by three main trends: trends which were represented by multifarious and diverse shades of opinions, but that were all well discernable.

The first trend of thought was represented by those national and loyalist elements who vigorously opposed the insupportable servilism of the Sztojai Government and who wanted to stop the inhuman actions surrounding the liquidation of the Jewish people. These same elements were opposed to the ever increasing shipments of staples and supplies to the Third Reich, which were causing a shortage in the country proper, and at the same time these elements demanded measures be taken to cope with the social situation and problems arising out of the war.

As a second current against these elements stood the extreme right wing circles, the "Imredist" movement and the great variety of the scatter groups of Hungarian National Socialists and their sympathizers.

The third trend was represented by groups which developed between the two above mentioned extremes. These were the so-called leftists: the democrats who realied upon the sympathies of the Anglo-Saxon powers, Socialists and Communists organizing under the influence of Soviet Russian propaganda, who conducted their activities in spite of the serious threat of persecution by the Gestapo.

Under the influence of the Hungarian Roman Catholic Church, the Protestant Clergy, the Holy See, and the Swedish and British rulers, and not in the least as a reflection of his own opinion, the Regent tried to get rid of the Sztojai Government. He desired to designate a new Cabinet which was to be headed by Geza Lakatos, a general called back to the capital from the eastern front. His intentions were no secret to the Germans, of course, and Veesenmayer read to him a rude and demanding letter from Hitler, in which he threatened to send two Panzer divisions to Hungary, and demanded the continuation of the Sztojai Government and that they serve the German interests in the future. At the same time, a coup d'état was planned by Baky in order to eliminate the Regent and kill Istvan Barczy, the Under Secretary of State of the Minister Presidency. The Regent, however, postponed the replacement of

Sztojai, stopped the deportation of the Jews, made a few changes in the Cabinet (namely having Imredy and his followers resign), and undertook a few measures for his personal security.

The situation at the front changed fundamentally. In June, the Anglo-Saxon powers landed in Normandy. In August, the Rumanians defected to the Russians, the Allies landed in Southern France, and the Soviet Russian Army fought in the foothills of the Carpathian Mountains, thrusting towards Rumania. That the Third Reich had lost the war was overpowering everywhere in Hungary. The population of Hungary was tormented by the nightmare of Soviet Russian terror and occupation and by the problem of how to avoid it. In the clear as to the difficulties of a solution to this problem were the Regent and his intimate inner circle, the broad political circles which also consisted of the Government Party, and the Democratic Socialist, and Small Holder Party elements of the so-called Peace Party. First of all, the German Army, which consisted of regular and SS units, held the most important strategical points of the country in their hands including all air fields. The Hungarian armed forces prepared for battle were fighting in the Carpathians defending the country. In the interior, inadequately armed and badly equipped Honved cadres represented merely mobilization centers. The Allies landing on the Balkan Peninsula, a much hoped for event by the Hungarians, never happened. The secret connections of the Hungarian Government with countries abroad were stopped because of the activities of the German intelligence and counter-intelligence. It was hopeless also to expect the arrival of Allied parachutists in the Transdanubian area. After the Rumanian defection to the Russians in August, the Hungarian-German front was broken through in the south by the Soviet Russian Army, and with the Rumanian units to bolster them, they threatened to inundate the Hungarian Plains through the gap in the line.

Under these circumstances the Regent and several serious minded politicians, called by the German sympathizers the "Palace clique," discussed the possibilities of an armistice as a means to avoid further bloodshed in this hopeless situation. First of all, Horthy insisted that the army units in the country proper be reinforced in order to be able to withstand eventual German atrocities and to this end, he ordered that in the mobilization areas of each division a so-called reserve division should be called to arms and form a reserve army. He recalled General Beregfi and placed his trustworthy Chief of the Military Cabinet General Bela Miklos in the commander's position of the First Hungarian Army, and nominated General Janos Vattay to head his Military Cabinet. He again toyed with the idea of replacing the Sztojai Government and of nominating a Cabinet consisting of a majority of soldiers who were above party politics. This intentions of his, however, was learned by the Germans through Winkelmann, and Hitler stopped it with a new rude, threatening letter. However, when Eichmann again demanded the shipping of Jews to Germany, the Regent threatened him with armed resistance and refused to comply with his request.

The defections of the Rumanians had its influence not only on the military situation but also in the inner political situation. Dissenting diplomats from abroad sent messages which expressed the Allied Power's opinion that it was necessary that the Hungarian Government follow the example of the Rumanian King Michael, and the Hungarian Ambassador at Ankara Voernle received similar advice from the English Ambassador in the same town. The Hungarian "Peace Party" and the left wing parties submitted memorandums to this effect to the Regent. The Germans, acting as if the Rumanian defection had shaken their self-reliance, began to adopt more understanding attitudes towards the Hungarian Government. Veesenmayer finally approved the substitution of Sztojai, and Himmler dropped the goal of controlling the personal property question of the Hungarian Jews and ordered Eichmann back to Germany. The German general staff, on the other hand, requested that Hungarian Army units should occupy the southern slopes of the Carpathians, which had been given at the Second Viennese Arbitrage to Rumania. Regent Horthy, however, was hesitant to take any of these steps for two reasons. First of all, he was reluctant to lay down arms solely and exclusively to the Soviet Russian Army, and then as a soldier and a gentleman he was reluctant to go behind his allies and commit treason. At a Cabinet meeting which was held in the absence of Sztojai, who was in the hospital for treatment, he had his standpoint accepted which was to oppose the occupation of the southern slopes of the Carpathians because if the Hungarian Army, which was still left in the country, were driven from there entirely, it would leave the country delivered to the whims of the Third Reich. Instead of implementing the requested actions, the Regent made a few precautions and postponing preparations. He asked the English Colonel Howie to visit him. Colonel Howie had escaped from a German prison camp in 1943 and was hiding in Hungary. The Regent asked him to get in touch, with the help of the secret radio transmitter hidden in the Royal Palace, with the Allies and respectively the English Army fighting in Italy. At the same time he signed Sztojai's resignation and began negotiations with Veesenmayer about the formation of the Lakatos Cabinet. This Government took over in late August 1944 and its members, with the exception of only two, were all loyal and reliable followers of Horthy. This Cabinet regarded its first task to free the Government and the public administration of those extremist elements who were members of the Arrow Cross Party or were German friends. Also, it wanted to finalize and solve the Jewish question forever by coming to an understanding with the Germans that the deportations were to be stopped and that Jews who were fit for military service should be inducted and should be utilized on public work projects, receiving regular pay; also that the property which had been confiscated from them should be inventoried and indemnity should be paid to them. The Government started negotiations with the Germans toward the release of deported and detained members of Parliament and Government officials, and decided to defend the Carpathian line against the Russians with all forces of the country.

Before Lakatos and his Government stood tremendous administrative questions: questions which arose out of the state of war, the Hungarian and German Armies, the industrial working capacity, and the public nutrition of the country and its cities, etc. Difficulties also arose out of the fact that the railroad lines were utilized to an excessive amount by the Army, and that the air raids had hit bridges, railroads, major arterials, highways, and industrial centers. Also, the collection of staples of food and other commodities required tremendous efforts of organization.

The political situation in August and September 1944 may be characterized as follows. The Government Party was unchanged in its loyalty. The Imredists, having lost their representation in the Government, maintained their relationships with the Germans but enveloped themselves in a great silence. The extreme right wing groups developed and strived for power and position, although Weesenmayer refrained from supporting them and the Government refused to deal with their demands. The left wing elements became more active. In secret they formed the "Hungarian Communist Party," and the latter entered into very close communication and relationship with the Social Democrats and even with some more extremist elements of the Small Holders Party. And not last was the "Peace Party." Upon the influence of the son of the Regent, Miklos Horthy Jr., this political group composed and submitted a memorandum to the Regent asking that he lay down arms to the Soviet Russians and that a Plenipotentiary be sent from Moscow to negotiate and to inform the Anglo-Saxon powers of his decisions. The Regent did not answer this memorandum.

In the course of the same months, great activity was conducted also in the foreign political sphere. Also Colonel Howie took up negotiations with the British through the radio. The only consequence of this was the immediate announcement by the Germans that they were going to direct artillery fire against Budapest if the secret radio transmitting continued. In spite of this, another secret message was sent to Prince Charles Louis in Lisbon, in which he was asked to interfere with the Western Powers and to request them to participate in the Hungarian negotiations pertaining to the laying down of arms in order that the Hungarians not be left alone with the Soviet Russians. This message was also relayed to Crown Prince Otto in the United States and he communicated the same to President Roosevelt. At the same time the dissident diplomat Bakach Bessenyei, a former ambassador then living in Switzerland, was entrusted to conduct negotiations with the Western Powers. As a result of the mission, he got in touch with Harrison, Ambassador of the United States to Switzerland, and from him he learned that the allied powers were demanding an unconditional surrender and that they did not want to exclude the Soviet Union from such negotiations; however, the American Ambassador and his British counterpart immediately requested orders from their respective governments, of course. Bessenyei reported all this to Budapest and requested also further orders.

During this time another important happening influenced Hungary's fate. General Heinz Guderian, the German Chief of Staff, arrived in Budapest. He negotiated with the Regent, with the Hungarian Minister of Defense, and the Chief of Staff. The result of these conferences was an agreement, according to which the Germans were going to lend support in the defense of the Hungarian frontiers, that the Hungarian armies which were fighting outside the country were to be concentrated in the country, and that the Hungarian Reserve Army Corps were going to be equipped with modern arms and sent to bolster the defenses. The negotiations also stated that in all these strategic military actions the frontier lines drawn at the Second Viennese Arbitrage did not have to be taken into consideration, meaning that the Hungarian Army units could take up defense positions anywhere in the southern Carpathians. Finally, they stated that the so-called "secret arms" were going to be also utilized in the defense of Hungary.

However, all of this happened otherwise. The derouted German Army did not stop in the Carpathian Mountain Chain but withdrew through the passes into the Hungarian Plains. The First Hungarian Army, to avoid an attack in her back, swung down to the Tisza River, and the Second and Third Hungarian Armies, hastily formed from the Reserve Army Corps with their obsolete equipment, were not strong enough to resist the overpowering enemy forces along the line of the Maros River and between the two rivers Tisza and the Danube. The unified Soviet Russian and Rumanian Armies now were thrusting towards the Great Hungarian Plains. All the Regent's hopes that the Soviet Russian armies could be stopped at the frontiers of the country tumbled down. To expect the arrival of Anglo-Saxon troops into Hungary was hopeless. Thus, the Regent and his circle of intimate counselors decided that negotiations ought to be entered into to arrange for an unconditional surrender, that they should try to establish certain important points as possible conditions: (a), the Allies would occupy in Hungary only strategically important points; (b), that the Rumanian and Yugoslav armies would not participate in the occupation; (c), that the Hungarian Administration might stay at their respective posts; and (d), that the German Army would be allowed to withdraw from Hungary. It was decided also that the request for surrender would be relayed through the Swedish and Turkish Embassies functioning in Hungary to the Western Powers to the effect that they should send out their representatives for negotiations. At the same time a wire was sent to Bessenyei which informed him that decisive steps for surrender would be undertaken on September 8. The Regent communicated his decisions and the chosen measures undertaken with the Council of Ministers; the Cabinet acknowledged the measures and also his decision to communicate, in a suitable form to Berlin, a request for surrender. This "suitable form" was that the Regent, upon advice of the Minister of Defense Csatay, directed a demand to the Germans to send within twenty-four hours five armored divisions to Hungary in support of the Hungarian Army fighting between the rivers Tisza and Danube, or otherwise Hungary would be obliged to request an armistice. The Regent also notified Hitler of this decision in a private letter. It was expected that the Germans would not be able to comply with the request of this "ultimatum," and in that case he would have a free hand in any negotiations taken up. But the situation formed itself again in an entirely different way. In the last minutes of this "ultimatum," the Germans notified General Lakatos, Prime Minister, that four German armored divisions are already on the way to Hungary and the fifth would arrive within a few days, and that several army divisions of the German Army fighting in the Balkans were going to thrust forward from the direction of Belgrade. All this taken into consideration, an immediate wire was sent to Bessenyei notifying him that the negotiations for an unconditional surrender had to be postponed to avoid an eventual civil war, and that Hungary was asking the help of Anglo-Saxon parachutist division.

The Soviet Russian Army gained impetus in its attack, in spite of the strong resistance of the Second and Third Hungarian Armies and that of the Wehrmacht, and it penetrated always further into the interior of Hungary. Political circles of the left wing, coupled with those of Transylvanian Parliamentary representatives, repeated their request for negotiations for an armistice, pointing out that the Allies had decided in Teheran that Hungary belonged in the Soviet Russian sphere of interest. The Lakatos Government threatened to abdicate and at a Crown Council, which consisted of former and new political personalities, the opinions were rather divergent as to the steps to be taken in this precarious situation. The Houses of Parliament, called together to listen to the inauguration speech of Minister President Lakatos at the end of September, decided to continue the war. Refugees which came from everywhere, from all parts of the country in Transdanubia, gave accounts of the terrible atrocities and debasing attitudes of the Soviet Russian armies.

In the midst of the entangled situation which had been complicated by opposing opinions, the Regent finally decided to take the initiative in his own hands. There were two possible ways to make Moscow cognizant of Hungary's stand in this situation and of the actions which she might undertake. There was the opportunity to request Count Wladimir Zichy, a large land owner in Slovakia, to get in touch with Russian intelligence agents operating in that country and to gather information through them. The second way was to make use of the services of Baron Ede Atzel, a large land owner in Transylvania, who declared that he was a member of the Communist party and would be inclined to travel to negotiate with Moscow. The Regent made use of the services of both of the above persons. Count Zichy soon reported that one of his men had traveled to Moscow and had come back with a reply from Stalin that he was ready to guarantee the territorial rights of Hungary in her present boundaries and that the Hungarian Army need not lay down her arms, that the Hungarian administration would continue to function, that the Rumanian troops fighting in Hungary were going to be withdrawn and also that he was ready to receive in Moscow a Hungarian delegation empowered to negotiate. Baron Atzel came back from Moscow and reported that Soviet Russian General Zukow would be ready to receive immediately a delegation consisting of three Hungarian plenipotentiaries if they were sent immediately to Moscow. Upon the receipt of this news, the Regent immediately communicated to our Ambassador in Sweden that he had decided to stop the state of war with the Russians and was going to send representatives to Moscow. He also asked the Ambassador to communicate these facts to the British, American, and the Russian Embassies. At the same time he sent General Naday and English Colonel Howie to Italy by airplane to negotiate with Lord Wilson, and English general, and to solicit the support of the English Government at the negotiations to be conducted with the Russians. Although these two above mentioned officers successfully reached Foggia in Italy and negotiated with Lord Wilson, they were unable to secure any success. At the same time Miklos Horthy Jr., without the knowledge of his father, sought contacts with Yugoslav General Tito (Joseph Broz), the leader of the Communists of that country, by making use of the good services of Felix Bornemissza, General Director of the Magyar Folyam és Tenger Hajózási Társaság (MFTR) [Translated into English: Hungarian River and Sea Shipping Company]. The results of his tragic attempts will be mentioned later in this study.

Now the Regent faced the difficult task of choosing his representatives to be sent to Moscow. This was a very difficult and rather delicate matter. His choice fell on Geza Teleki, son of the former Hungarian Minister President Count Pal Teleki, and Gendarmerie General Sandor Faragho, the latter having been military attaché of our country to Moscow in the early Forties. These two gentlemen, having been furnished with all necessary directives and papers, started their travels to Moscow on the 28th of September in greatest secrecy. Accounts of the results of the negotiations conducted by General Faragho were relayed in his several secret radio messages. According to these, immediately after his arrival Faragho negotiated first with General Krzniezov, deputy chief of staff of the Russian General Staff, and later with General Antonov, chief of staff of the Soviet Russian General Staff. Both refused to negotiate for anything except the military aspects of the armistice. Faragho requested that in compliance with the previous messages received through Count Zichy, the political questions surrounding the armistice ought to be negotiated also. As a result of his demand, Foreign Commissar Molotov received Faragho twice and communicated to him that the reports of Count Zichy were not to be regarded as official; the preliminary conditions of an Armistice as stipulated with the consent of the Anglo-Saxon powers were the following.

Hungary was to withdraw immediately from the territories she occupied in Czechoslovakia, Rumania, and Yugoslavia, withdrawing within her boundaries prior to the two Viennese Arbitrage decisions. She was to immediately break connections with the Germans and to declare war on the Third Reich. When Faragho had obtained Molotov's consent to a concentration of all Hungarian battle groups toward Budapest and to the cessation of the air raids directed against the capital and had also received full power from the Regent, he signed on October 11 the protocols containing the above enumerated conditions; he reported this fact to the Regent with the request that a commanding general be sent to the Soviet Russians to negotiate about the details. The Regent, who regarded the request for the armistice as one of his constitutional rights, had a proclamation worked out in which he communicated the laying down of arms and the request for an armistice by the Hungarian nation.

While these secret negotiations and actions went on in the innermost secret circles surrounding the Regent during September and the first days of October 1944, the Germans also prepared in the greatest secrecy for counter action to prevent an eventual defection by the Hungarians. German Ambassador Veesenmayer negotiated several times with Ferenc Szalasi, head of the Hungarian Arrow Cross of Nazi Party, and thought that eventually an armed group of the latter headed by Emil Kovarcz could be utilized against the Regent and the Hungarian Government. SS General Winkelmann, on the other hand, was more inclined to make us, if it was necessary, of the Keleti Arcvonal Bajtársi Szövetség (K.A.B.Sz) [English translation: Collegiate

Federation of the Fighters of the Eastern Front]. This group was politically close to Imredy and was well trained and well equipped. Hitler sent SS Major Skorzeny to Budapest. This man had played an extremely outstanding role in the escape of Mussolini from his place of detention in the Italian Gran-Sassa. He came with his own special battle group to begin orientation and, in case it was necessary, to arrest the Regent. Veesenmayer preferred to take the smooth and possibly mild way for a change and to reach his goal eventually by use of constitutional steps. Winkelmann wanted to put terror actions and worse methods into swing. To decide between these two German factions, they both traveled to Berlin to ask directives from Hitler, Ribbentropp, and Himmler. During their absence Szalasi worked out a detailed plan for the removal of the Regent and the takeover of power. He worked out a complete re-orientation and transformation of the Hungarian Administration, and he compiled a list for the future Cabinet and also a list to replace the commanding generals; and all this in the interest of the continuation of the war on the side of the Germans provided the latter would support the defense of Hungary honestly and with all their power. He expected to carry out these plans toward the middle of November 1944.

In the meantime, in the political sphere there occurred two very important events. One: the formation of the "Nemzeti Szövetség" [Translated: National Federation] by Ferenc Rajniss, a member of Parliament and of the Government Party. This Federation counted over 200 Parliamentarians among its members very quickly; it decided to continue the war and did not want to break down relationships with the Third Reich, and they wanted to find constitutional ways to the solution of the problems created by the ever-increasing pressure exercised on political life by the Arrow Cross Party. The group reported its foundation, its aims and its requests to Minister President Lakatos and to the Regent. At the same time Miklos Horthy Jr. started a new "resistance movement," forming it out of the ranks of the Small Holder and Social Democratic Parties and those of the so-called "Peace Party." This latter group sent a memorandum to the Regent in which they proposed to create a democratic government, and also requested the release of political prisoners, the armament of the workers, and a cooperation with the Soviet Russian Army.

At the same time, in the military field, General Szilard Bakay, the Commander of the First and Second Reserve Army Corps, and General Karoly Lazar, commanding the garrison of the capital city of Budapest and also the body guard of the Regent, organized forces to be utilized in the eventual case of German atrocities. General Bakay had a few Nazis arrested, although he released them later upon the intervention by Veesenmayer. Shortly after this incident, General Bakay was captured one night by armed National Socialists and taken to Germany. He regained his freedom after the end of the war.

Veesenmayer and Winkelmann only returned to Budapest in the first part of October. They kept the result of their negotiations conducted in Berlin the greatest secret, even in front of Szalasi, but their attitude made it perceptible that Hitler must have decided to eliminate the Regent. The German newspapers started to brand the various Hungarian Governments as weak and cowardly and that the Third Reich was going to see to it that their activities should not hamper the progress of the war. Veesenmayer conducted lengthy and frequent negotiations with Szalasi and his staff concerning the implementation of their plans. But he was rather careful because of the hated character of Szalasi. Winkelmann wanted to have quick and efficient actions immediately. His plan was to gather in Estergom all the adherents of Szalasi, Szalasi himself, and also to be summoned there was the Hungarian Parliament which would have then to pronounce the removal of the Regent and the transfer of the powers of head of state to Szalasi.

But apparently in Berlin they did not have the confidence in Veesenmayer nor in Winkelmann to be the skillful personalities to carry out such a complicated plan of great delicacy, namely, to observe constitutional appearances in making a change. Therefore, Hitler sent SS General Von Dem Bach-Zalevsky from Warsaw and special ambassador and advisor to Mussolini, Rudolf Rahn from Carnago, Italy, to Budapest with special powers over and above the three SS battalions and Gestapo units already under the command of Skorzeny. Rahn received orders to solve the problem if possible with peaceful negotiations with the Regent. Von Dem Bach-Zalevsky, however, was empowered to use any means, even terror actions. This German apparatus was ready to strike on October 14. Veesenmayer requested an audience with the Regent for October 15 in order to make a last attempt accompanied by Rahn to prevent the Regent from committing treason.

According to the sources of information and also according to his own memoirs, in those days the Regent decided to undertake decisive and final steps to solve the problems and the climax fell exactly on October 14. He had a proclamation worked out through his chief of Civilian Cabinet Office Gyula Ambrozy, in which he intended to communicate to the nation that he was asking for an armistice. He also transmitted the text of the proclamation to Minister President Lakatos who in turn read it and submitted it to the Council of Ministers. There, all ministers with the exception of two agreed with the stand and were of the opinion that, as the chief of the Army, the Regent had the right to request and proclaim an armistice on his own constitutional powers. The Regent also decided that at twelve o'clock on October 15 he was going to receive Veesenmayer, the German Ambassador, and he would communicate to him the

text of the proclamation which would have then been immediately broadcast in several foreign languages through the
Hungarian radio network. He wanted at the same time to direct
coded wireless messages to General Miklos and General Veress,
commanding the First and Second Armies respectively. These
messages would have given them the directives about what to
do to carry out the armistice. He entrusted the development of
a defense position in the capital to General Ferenc Farkas,
also entrusted the task of keeping order in the capital city to
General Aggteleki, and finally, entrusted the defense of the
fortress in Buda to General Lazar. The Regent also communicated his intentions about the armistice to these above mentioned
generals, and he communicated his intentions to Chief of the
Hungarian General Staff General Janos Voros too. The latter
tried to influence the Regent to place himself under the protection of the First Hungarian Army and pointed out the great
difficulties and threatening dangers of the planned decisive
action.

During the night of the 14th and 15th of October, Colonel
Geza Utassy, who was sent by the Regent to Szeged, got in
touch with Soviet Russian Marshall Malinovski, commander of
the Armies thrusting forward from the Balkans. He returned
and brought with him the conditions of the armistice. These
were that the Hungarian connections had to be broken off with
the Germans within 48 hours, that the Germans had to be
attacked immediately, and that the Hungarian Army would
withdraw from the territories which she held in Czechoslovakia,
Rumania, and Yugoslavia. Malinovski also requested that a
report on the situation be rendered to him at his headquarters
in Szeged on October 16. This ultimatum in reality was merely
a repetition of the conditions which had been communicated a
few days before through General Faragho to the Regent and
received as such from Molotov. Horthy, however, received his
reports in the morning of October 15.

But on this fateful morning of October 15, the Regent received several other disturbing and dramatic news. The Hungarian Chief of Staff Janos Voros received, at about ten o'clock
of the same day, an ultimatum from German Chief of General
Staff Guderian, according to which from then on Hungary was
to be regarded as a German strategic territory in which the
Hungarian Army could receive orders only and exclusively from
the German High Command and that all orders issued by the
Hungarian Army were void and null. Guderian also communicated that the new German Panzer divisions are enroute
to reinforce the northeastern front. Also in these same hours
the news came to the Royal Palace that Miklos Horthy Jr. had
been caught by Skorzeny's henchmen at about nine in the
morning while negotiating in the offices of the Magyar Folyam
és Tenger Hajózási Társaság [Hungarian River and Sea Shipping Company] with representatives of Marshall Tito. Whether

82

this had been a genuine representative or a German agent is unknown as of yet. The chauffeur and the car in which he had arrived were dynamited, one of his friends was shot in the stomach, and he was bludgeoned, wrapped in a blanket and taken in a fast car to the airport where he was immediately shipped to Germany. (I mentioned this happening earlier in my study.)

These were the circumstances under which the Regent at 10:30 a.m. opened the Crown Council summoned for that day. Only a few members of Cabinet and a few outstanding political personalities were participating. The Regent communicated to them the happenings of the morning, described the attitude of the Third Reich towards Hungary and revealed that as a consequence of those factors he had decided to request an armistice. After the Regent's statement, Chief of the General Staff Voros and Minister President Lakatos gave reports about the futility of a defeated military situation. In the meantime, the clock showed noon and, adjourning the Crown Council, the Regent withdrew to another room to receive Veesenmayer. There he made bitter reproaches to the German Ambassador, mentioning the arrest of General Bakay and that of his own son, and he told him that he was not going to continue the war and that he was going to request an armistice. Veesenmayer showed great surprise and proposed that the Regent should also hear Rahn. The Regent acceded to his wishes but did not tell Veesenmayer that he had already undertaken all the steps and measures to request an armistice. After Veesenmayer's visit he also forgot to give the orders for the broadcasting of the proclamation, but when he returned to the room of the Crown Council, he ordered that the proclamation be communicated to the commanding generals of the First and Second Armies. All this resulted in technical troubles and delays, and the radio broadcast the proclamation at 1:00 p.m. rather than at 12:30 p.m. and repeated it several times in several foreign languages. In the meantime, the Government Printing Office produced the place-cards of the proclamation but they were never distributed.

During the first broadcast of the proclamation, Rahn arrived at the Royal Palace and the Regent received him immediately. In a stormy dialogue lasting more than an hour, the Regent repeated his reproaches concerning the attitudes of the Third Reich, and Rahn proposed the question of how Horthy proposed to avoid bloodshed between the Germans, the Soviet Russians, and his own opposition party, the Arrow Crossers. The Regent saw only one way out of this: that was that the German Army withdrew behind the Austrian frontiers. According to Rahn this would have been possible only if the Hungarians would not lay down their arms to the Russians, and if they would not stand to the side of the Russians, but in either case armed clashes between Hungarians and Germans were possible. The conversation and negotiations terminated with a promise by Rahn to report everything to Hitler and to ask directives; the Regent promised Rahn that he would take his propositions into consideration.

During this time, Foreign Minister Hennyei communicated to the Swedish and Turkish Embassies in Budapest the proclamation and its reasons, and communicated also to the Hungarian Embassies in Stockholm and Ankara the request that they should bring the facts to the attention of the representatives of the Allied Powers.

After Rahn's departure, the Regent again opened the Crown Council, and now the Lakatos Government formally abdicated. The Regent designated that the abdicated ministers, with the exception of two (Jurcsek and Remenyi-Schneller), form a new Government and continue carrying on the affairs. The new Government took the oath at 3 p.m. The afternoon was characterized by two new developments in addition to the above. After his audience with the Regent, Rahn returned to the German Embassy where he discussed in detail his conversation with Horthy with Ambassador Veesenmayer. They decided that Hitler would quite probably not accede to the wish to withdraw the German Army from Hungary, and that Horthy would quite probably not change his plans pertaining to the request of an armistice; therefore, forced action would quite probably not be avoidable.

After having ascertained that their opinions were congruent, they got in touch with Von Dem Bach-Zalevsky and the three German plenipotentiaries decided to remove the Regent and replace him with Szalasi. Through this action they wanted to prevent the Hungarian Army from stopping her actions against the Russians and turning against the Germans. They also decided that before the Panzerfaust [Translated: Ironfist] operation started, a renewed attempt would be made to carry out in a peaceful manner this change of leading personalities. For these actions the SS General gave a deadline until six o'clock of the morning of October 16.

At the same time that all this happened, the staff officers at the operation division of the Hungarian General Staff listened with great concern to the proclamation of the Regent; they obtained orders to carry out the stipulations of the same from the hands of Chief of Staff Voros. Their surprise was of course genuine because they had not known about the Regent's decision and could not have prepared any measures or orders to the Army fighting on the front or stationed in their various garrisons. The situation became even more entangled when Voros arrived at his office and immediately denied knowledge of the proclamation and also denied that he would have signed orders to effect the carrying out its stipulations. However, later he proved to be a two-faced player, for then he repeated again and again that the proclamation issued by the Regent as Commander in Chief of the Army must be carried out. At the time that a very heated debate had developed as to the implementation of the order, Veesenmayer burst into the room and, referring to his conversation with the Regent, demanded that Voros should immediately issue counter orders to void the previous ones issued. Voros promised this and, after Veesenmayer's departure, discussed the necessary actions with his subordinate officers and had the following orders written out: "Nobody should interpret the statements heard in the radio speech of the Regent as a surrender of the Hungarian Army. At present the question is only to negotiate an armistice. Therefore, since the outcome of these negotiations is unknown, all Hungarian units should continue fighting with unchanged effort against all attacks." These orders were issued at about 5 p.m. with the signature of Voros and sent to all fighting and garrisoned units.

These stormy events resulted in a series of misunderstandings, hasty actions, and contradictory measures which caused turmoils. General Miklos, the commander of the First Army, was not at his headquarters at Huszt and heard the proclamation of the Regent over the radio at Beregszasz. He immediately issued an order that the units subordinate to him should cease hostilities with the Russians and should attack the Germans. But nobody followed his orders, since they had received in the meantime the countermanding order of the Chief of the General Staff Voros. When Miklos returned to Huszt and learned about the rescinding order, he of course was obliged to withdraw his previous orders. Janos Veress, Commanding General of the Second Hungarian Army, was in heavy battle with the Soviet Russians at the time and neither heard nor received orders concerning the proclamation of the Regent or the countermanding orders of Voros; therefore, he continued his tactical moves. General Heszlenyi, the commander of the Third Hungarian Army, heard the proclamation of the Regent but did not act upon it. The garrisons remained inactive. Only the commander of the garrison in Budapest, General Aggteleki, introduced a few measures to maintain law and order. These measures, however, because of the very small resources of his armed contingencies proved to be very ineffective. Although the Germans tried to stop the adherents of Szalasi from any hasty actions, one of their leaders Kovarcz succeeded in overpowering by ruse the officers of the Magyar Távirati Iroda [Translated: Hungarian Telegraph Office] and also the radio station of Laki Hegy. Von Dem Bach-Zalevski was satisfied by only sending his armored cars and patrols overnight into the streets of Budapest. The population of Budapest, just as that of the country towns and villages, continued their routine daily activities with great inertia and only very sporadically were there some elements of the youth shouting slogans.

After having taken the oath, the members of the new Cabinet returned to the Palace of the Minister President. There, on the basis of reports coming in from every sector of the country, they learned that the Hungarian Army was not going to follow the orders of the Regent, that the commander in charge of the defense of Budapest, General Aggteleki, had been arrested by his own officers and that Kovarcz had taken over the radio. They also learned that the capital city was under the rule of Szalasi and that the latter was plotting with the Germans to take over the Government. Thus, the Cabinet decided to get in touch with the German representatives and try and save whatever was left to be saved. Minister President Lakatos telephoned to Veesenmayer and Rahn, requesting them to appear at the Minister Presidency. The latter did not accede to his wishes because they were suspicious of an eventual trap. Therefore, they requested Lakatos to come to the German Embassy. However, he was reluctant to accept this invitation, being fearful of eventual meddling by Szalasi. Finally they decided that Veesenmayer would send one of the Legation cars and, as an escort, one of the secretaries of the German Legation to fetch the Minister President. Upon this, Lakatos, accompanied by the Minister of Foreign Affairs Hennyei, went to the German Embassy where he discussed the situation at length with Veesenmayer in the presence of Rahn, and also discussed the possibilities of a peaceful evolution. In view of the fact that the Hungarian Army had compiled to the agreement reached between the Regent and Rahn and had not surrendered but had continued to fight, the Hungarian representatives demanded that the German Army withdraw to the Austrian frontier, that General Bakay and Miklos Horthy Jr. be set free, and also emphasized that the Regent was unshakable in his decision to enter armistice negotiations. Thinking that the rigid attitude of the Regent would change pretty soon, the two German diplomats tried to postpone and stretch out the negotiations, stating that they were ready to report the Hungarian demands to Hitler and they wanted them in writing. At that very moment a German officer entered and reported that General Lazar had ordered that all streets leading into the fortress be closed by mine fields. This came as an excellent point for delay to the Germans, and they immediately stated that they did not wish to continue with negotiations any more because they regarded themselves as prisoners. They asked the Hungarians to leave the offices of the Embassy immediately. At the same time, Minister of Defense Csatay received a telegram message from Von Dem Bach-Zalewski who said that if General Lazar did not eliminate all the mines by 8:00 p.m., the SS was going to storm the fortress. Also at the very same moment Ribbentropp telephoned Veesenmayer, and in utmost anger reprimanded him for his delaying attitude and actions, relieved him of his duties and ordered him to report with Rahn at the general headquarters of General Greiffenberg at the Svabhegy in order to be placed under arrest.

On the other hand, during these same afternoon hours the

Regent negotiated with General Voros, Chief of Staff, and Colonel Nadas, Chief of the Tactical Division of the General Staff, about sending a delegation headed by Colonel Utassy to Soviet Russian General Malinowsky at Szeged. The delegation should have negotiated about the modalities of the surrender. During these negotiations, the aide-de-camp Toszt reported that the Germans intended to attack the fortress and he requested the Regent to hurry into the air raid shelter. Utassy never reached Szeged for he was arrested in the course of the same night.

In the meantime, the Minister President returned to his office and there summed up in an aide memoire the Hungarian request discussed at the German Legation while the men of Von Dem Bach-Zalewski and Skorzeny occupied all Danube bridges and the streets leading into the fortress and other tactically important points. They made preparations for their attack which was planned to start at six o'clock the following morning. Szalasi and his party constantly broadcast their slogans over the radio.

It may have been around ten o'clock when the Regent requested the presence of Lakatos, of the Ministers Hennyei and Rakovszky, and also that of Chief of Staff General Voros. The Ministers hurried immediately to Horthy but Voros refused to go. The Regent communicated to the Ministers that he had received an ultimatum from General Antinov, Chief of the Soviet Russian General Staff, and according to it the conditions of the surrender had to be accepted by 4 a.m. on October 16, which was the next day, or else all negotiations would be stopped immediately. The Regent asked Foreign Minister Hennyei to formulate an answer. The Ministers were very surprised by the news of such an ultimatum because they had not be cognizant of the negotiations conducted by General Faragho in Moscow. Only after Ambrozy, Chief of the Regent's Civilian Cabinet, had explained the background to them, the preceding happenings, and the steps that had been taken, did they decide to communicate to Antinov that they had broken all connections with the Germans and that as further steps to be taken, they were requesting that Antinov get in touch with the commanding generals of the First and Second Hungarian Armies. After this the Ministers returned to the Minister Presidency. Then in a moment of desperation Minister President Lakatos telephoned Veesenmayer to communicate the happenings to him and to ask him to do everything to avoid mutual bloodshed. The German Ambassador gave an evasive answer. In the meantime, General Vattay, chief of the Regent's Military Cabinet, arrived at the Minister Presidency and communicated to the Ministers that the armed attack by the Germans was about to break at any minute and that the life of the Regent was in danger. The only way out of the situation that he could see was that the Regent be taken prisoner of war and that the

Cabinet turn the Government over to the Germans after which Hungary would no longer be regarded a free state. The Ministers were in favor of Vattay's proposals and upon this the General returned to the Regent in order to persuade him to accept the same fate. In spite of the persuasive efforts of Vattay, Ambrozi, and the two aides-de-camp, the Regent and his family refused to accept those proposals. Vattay returned to the Minister Presidency and stated that the Regent had accepted his proposals; he persuaded the Minister to telephone and inform the German Embassy that in order to avoid bloodshed and a civil war the Hungarian Government was abdicating, and that the Regent had decided to withdraw and was asking for asylum in the German Reich. This message was taken at 2 a.m. by Feine, Secretary of the German Legation, with the pronouncement that Veesenmayer would immediately relay the message to Hitler. At about four in the morning, General Lazar reported to the Regent that the German SS troops were preparing to attack at 6 a.m. The Regent ordered him to resist to the last man and also ordered that his family be placed in the protection of the Palace of the Apostolic Nuncio. The SS started to attack the fortress; one battalion of the defense units commanded by General Lazar defected to them. The General regrouped his forces and the shooting began. Minister President Lakatos notified General Lazar at five in the morning that he had received a consent to compromise and that the fighting should cease immediately. Lazar did not believe the message and continued to resist. During this time Lakatos, accompanied by Veesenmayer, had arrived at the Royal Palace. General Vattay, who was in attendance of the Regent, persuaded him to receive Veesenmayer. This happened and Veesenmayer made the following statement: "I have the disagreeable task of placing your Serenissime in safety because our attack is going to start in a few minutes." Upon the question of the Regent as to where he was going, Veesenmayer answered, "to the Hatvany Palace," and taking him by the arm, led him away; during this conversation orders were issued to Lazar to cease hostilities. Lakatos, Vattay, and the aides-de-camp Toszt and Brunswick followed them. The SS, however, continued their attack and penetrated the Royal Palace where they captured General Lazar and started to deracinate and annihilate the chambers. Several Hungarian and German victims were wounded and died in the armed resistance. Ministers Hennyei, Rakovszky, and Schell were arrested and taken to the jail located in the Foucca. In the Hatvany Palace the Regent was separated from his suite and was placed in one room, while Lakatos, Vattay, and the two aides-de-camp were placed in another room. Both were guarded by armed SS men. There Toszt shot himself to death fearing that the Germans would force him to betray top secrets.

In the meantime, Veesenmayer started to form a new Government under the leadership of Szalasi, and he invited the prospective members of this Cabinet to the German Embassy. There he communicated to Szalasi that the Regent wanted to see him. This was untrue; however, Szalasi, believing that he was to receive the Regent's order to form a new Government, reported to the latter, only to have Horthy deny him an audience. Then Minister President Lakatos was taken under an armed escort to the German Legation where in the presence of Rahn and the Secretary of the Legation Feine, Veesenmayer communicated to him that only if the Regent retracted his proclamation, abdicated from his office, and designated Szalasi Minister President, would Hitler treat Horthy in a manner deserved by a head of state. Lakatos returned to the Hatvany Palace and reported these conditions to the Regent. He was willing to retract his proclamation and signed a document prepared in German. The contents were approximately the following: "I declare that my proclamation dated October 15 is invalid and I am repeating the orders of the Chief of the General Staff that the fighting has to be relentlessly continued." Lakatos took this document to the German Embassy stating that the Regent refused to comply with the two other conditions. After this he was taken back to the jail located in the Foucca where an SS officer gave him a pass according to which he was allowed to return to his home located in the Minister Presidency. At seven in the morning, he was summoned again from there to the German Embassy where he was told that Veesenmayer and Rahn personally had tried to persuade the Regent to abdicate and to nominate Szalasi but that Horthy had refused to accede to their wishes and to sign the pertinent documents and consequently both his own life and his son's were in real danger. Lakatos and Rahn drew up now another document which contained the abdication of the Regent in constitutional form and also the designation of Szalasi. This document was taken by Lakatos and Veesenmayer to the Regent's residence where Horthy had been taken under an armed guard to pack certain things for travel. When the two gentlemen explained to the Regent the contents of the document, his only question was, "What is going to happen to my son?" Upon this Veesenmayer answered, "I obtained orders from the highest place that he is going to be taken tomorrow to Vienna and set free." Upon this the Regent signed the document emphasizing that he was doing such only under duress and it could not be regarded as legally valid. The document was addressed to the presidents of the two Houses of Parliament and contained approximately the following: "I am abdicated from my office of Regent and of my rights as Regent and designate Ferenc Szalasi to form a united national government. Dated October 16, 1944." The signing of the document happened at 8:15 in the morning and the document was taken over for safe keeping by Veesenmayer.

In the afternoon hours Miklos Horthy was escorted by the

henchmen of Skorzeny to the railroad station of Kelenfold where he was joined by his family consisting of his wife, his daughter-in-law, his grandson, and the Generals Vattay and Brunswick. The Regent and his family were placed under rigid guard in the Castle of Hirschberg near the Bavarian city of Weilheim. Miklos Horthy Jr. did not join the family at Vienna nor at Linz. The Germans, not keeping their promises, placed him in the concentration camp of Mauthausen after he recuperated from his wounds, and later transferred him to Dachau. Later Vattay and Brunswich were also interned somewhere.

Here I would like to mention two important characteristic happenings which illustrate the situation in Hungary. Bela Miklos, commanding general of the First Hungarian Army, was ordered to appear at the headquarters of General Heinritzi, commander of the German Army Group, on October 16. Miklos, suspicious of an eventual arrest, defected through the Hungarian front with one of his aides and two sergeants to the Soviet Russians who after his apprehension escorted him to Lisko, near Prsemysl, to their general headquarters where he arrived in the morning of October 17. In compliance with the requests of the Soviet Russians, he spoke on the radio and asked the commanding officers of his Army that they come over to the Soviet Russians with their units, for the Russians would rearm the Hungarian prisoners of war and out of them they would form a liberation army. With the exception of only one regimental commander who was arrested by the Germans and immediately executed, nobody followed the petition of Miklos. A few days later emissaries were sent to negotiate with Miklos about the formation of a Hungarian counter-Government, but without any results. His counter-Government was formed only in 1945 in Debrecen. On October 21 he again spoke by radio to the Hungarian soldiers telling them they should defect to the Soviet Russians. This resulted in several persons defecting their units, however, not to the Russians but simply returning to their homelands.

At this time the Moscow radio started to call Janos Voros, Chief of the General Staff, advising him to defect to the Soviet Russians because the Germans were going to hang him. Voros defected to the Russians on October 31 at Szeged, and later spoke over the radio from Moscow to the Hungarian nation and asked them to surrender.

I do not want to talk about the political and military happenings during the six months rule of the Szalasi Government. The only decisive factor was that with his foreign methods, foreign principles, and service of foreign interests, he was unable to stop the tragic fate of Hungary.

Chapter II

SECRET DIPLOMATIC RELATIONS

Prior to the Treaty of Trianon Hungary did not have an independent foreign policy. All diplomatic activities were so-called mutual affairs of the Austro-Hungarian Monarchy and based upon an agreement reached in 1867 with the Austrian Empire in the frame of the compromise. All foreign affairs were led by the Imperial and Royal Ministry of Foreign Affairs in compliance to the interests of the Monarchy as a major power of the world. These interests were not necessarily identical with Hungary's. This is a fact which is by now known all over the world and which was illustrated by the Minister President of Hungary Count Istvan Tisza's protests in 1914 against the declaration of war against Serbia.

After the signing of Trianon peace treaty on June 4, 1920, the foreign policy of the new "independent" Hungary under the changed geopolitical auspices of Europe consisted of seeking the means and ways to change the inhuman regulations of the Treaty of Trianon which threatened a slow death to the country's existence.

Let us make a brief survey of the changed situation in Europe, but from the Hungarian viewpoint, however.

To the east of the mutilated and unprotected Hungary the Soviet Russian Empire began to organize and, after her diplomatic successes of 1935 when she was accepted as a member of the League of Nations, she developed her Communist imperialistic intrigues. At the time these matters did not affect Hungary.

To the west stood the Entente which consisted of the English and the French who had constructed the systems of the peace treaties signed at Paris. Also there was the Little Entente which consisted of Czechoslovakia, Rumania, and Yugoslavia who aimed to enforce the stipulations of the peace treaties and enforce and strengthen the *status quo*. They definitely formed a hostile ring around the country.

Also in the west was the new German Republic created on the debris of the German Empire. Political and economic crises were the order of the day in that country. Our immediate neighbor, Imperial Austria, changed and became the Austrian Federated Republic whose political and economic future was rather difficult. Both these countries were of dubious value in any foreign political relationship.

To the north there was Poland who began to develop once she had surmounted the problems of entangled territorial questions; Hungary had enjoyed friendly relations with Poland for several centuries and it was firmly hoped in those days that Poland would enter into favorable foreign relations with Hungary once she was able to organize and stabilize her internal and external situation.

To the south Hungary was barred from Bulgaria, Turkey and Greece by the hostile countries of Rumania and Yugoslavia. All three, Bulgaria, Turkey, and Hungary, suffered in the First World War on the losing side. Bulgaria still had some disagreeable, unsolved territorial questions with Rumania and Yugoslavia; on the other hand, Turkey secured outstanding diplomatic successes in 1923 at Lausanne which, of course, would have been of great interest also to Hungary. A relationship with Greece, who had great internal troubles, seemed to be of no particular interest or value.

Also to the south was Italy. There, Mussolini was successfully putting down all internal turmoils but neither was he satisfied with the stipulations of the peace treaties (especially in territorial respects), and he was cognizant of other shortcomings of the forced regulations. He had already manifested his friendly feelings toward Hungary by 1921.

In the ten or twelve years following the signing of the Treaty of Trianon, Hungary's diplomatic activities in the general European scene were limited to a great extent. Soon, however, there were favorable signs for possible revisions. For instance, in 1921, by popular suffrage the old Hungarian town of Sopron, which had been allocated to Austria by the Treaty of Trianon, was returned to the mother country. In the same year the Minister President of France, Millerand, communicated to the Hungarian Government in a note that there were possibilities for the modification of the selected clauses of the Treaty of Trianon. It had been proven in 1923 at the international conference held at Lausanne that the peace treaties could be changed. Aristotle Briand, French Minister President, also followed this trend, and planned the formation of the federation of the Danube countries. In 1927, in a major public speech, Mussolini emphasized Hungary's right to a revision of the Treaty of Trianon, and he soon concluded a friendship pact between Hungary and Italy. Hungary received loans from the League of Nations at Geneva in 1921 and also in 1930. In 1931 a friendship pact was concluded between Hungary and Austria. The Hungarian foreign policy and diplomacy made use exclusively of classic methods of approach in her efforts to change the opinions towards the peace treaties: namely, she addressed notes to the various countries. The influential powers, however, were impressed tremendously by the general staff of the Little Entente: Benes of Prague, Titulescu of Bucharest, and Pasic of Belgrad; and these powers formed the opinion that Hungary was serving German imperialistic aims. The Hungarian diplomats were rather careful about the wording of these notes, especially since they realized that in the eyes of the Entente Cordiale the credibility of the Little Entente was unshakeable. In Hungary, it is a well-known fact that the Little Entente used all the back doors to get into the government offices of Paris, London, and Washington; that it officially and unofficially disseminated distorted news about Hungary with great success, and for money the press in almost every country was entirely at their service. The Hungarian Government was reluctant to follow a similar road; who knows whether it was out of caution, fear, or inexperience, or hope for justice. Neither did the Hungarian Government follow the example of Poland, Bulgaria, Turkey, Germany, or Italy even though they did prove that with tenacity and endurance great successes can be attained. The Hungarian Government was under the constant pressure of public opinion and could not table the demands for a revision of the Trianon peace treaties: the revision, of course, was the sole logical aim of the Hungarian foreign policies. But the Government did nothing which was particularly auspicious to reach such an aim. They always moved in circles. They did not even make a concentrated effort to develop Hungary's military defenses.

Two major facts later changed these trends of the Hungarian foreign policy. One was that Count Istvan Bethlen as Minister President led the country for ten years on the so-called "Golden Middle Road," as he and his followers named it. Then in 1933 Adolf Hitler took over the power in Germany and with this act the political atmosphere of Europe underwent radical changes.

In 1932 Gyula Gombos moved into the chair of Minister President. He recognized the great dangers which were threatening the country; to the east there was the ever increasing power of Soviet Russia, and to the west there was the newly formed Third Reich with its imperialistic tendencies. He decided that he would attempt to defend the country efficiently against both of these. He selected neither the approach of under cover agents and bribe nor intrigue; instead, he openly began laying the foundations for a defense alliance to be headed by Italy, and negotiated with Austria, Poland, Bulgaria, Turkey, and even with Yugoslavia. He also tried to gain France's approval for a reorganization of the Hungarian Army. He paid two visits to Hitler which gave him the opportunity to sound out the intentions of the "Führer" and these findings fortified his actions and efforts to develop a defense block. His personal negotiations conducted in Vienna, Rome, and Ankara, and the steps undertaken upon his initiative by our legations in Warsaw, Sophia, and Belgrad became known throughout the world through the news media.

It was Gombos' successor, Minister President Kalman Daranyi, who was in charge of the country's affairs when the Anschluss was carried out in March 1938; these actions left no doubts as to the ruthless methods and intentions of Hitler, especially after details of the happenings at the Hossbach Conference became known. Daranyi quietly evaluated the situation and foresaw the immense dangers accumulating, but also noticed that the Entente had not tried to avert this danger or prevent it even after the occupation of the Ruhr country. The formation of the defense block of countries started by Gombos became a futile dream because of the seizure of Austria. Italy also oriented her policies more and more in the direction of the Third Reich, and the Danube Confederation of countries, also promoted by Mussolini, suffered shipwreck due to the attitudes of the French Government. Daranyi's foreign policy was limited to the performance of activities which he did not welcome: paying visits to Berlin to secure certain economic benefits for Hungary, and leaving the Italian affairs to his Minister of Foreign Affairs Kanya. Reluctantly he also followed the Italian and German examples of establishing an approach to Yugoslavia. He did not try to gain the sympathies of the Entente but, after having delivered a major speech concerning the economic life of the country at the city of Gyor, he made steps towards developing Hungary's armed forces.

It was during the term of office of his successor, Bela Imredy, a liberal, mercantilist, that the Munich Conference and the First Viennese Arbitrage decisions took place. Both these events indicate that the Entente was only slightly oriented to the preparatory move made by Hitler, and indicate also that the Little Entente held political and military positions of no great importance. At the same time there arose great hopes in Hungary that through actions of the Third Reich she would eventually regain territories that had been detached from the mother country by the Treaty of Trianon. Imredy, who even sent commercial attachés to the Hungarian Embassy in London, soon became aware of the fact that Berlin and Rome did not trust him. He shifted his policies towards the totalitarian systems (Author's remark: later its political motives became quite obvious). He never initiated any effective policies towards the western powers or powers overseas, and his diplomatic activities were limited to paying visits to Hitler and Mussolini and to legislation concerning the Jews.

In February 1939, Count Pal Teleki took over the Minister Presidency; this outstanding Hungarian statesman, with his immense scientific background and knowledge, clearly saw the dangers of the Third Reich's imperialistic drives but he also knew the weaknesses of the West. He wanted to make use of the German tendencies to make gains in Hungarian territorial questions but at the same time he wanted to persuade the Entente powers of the justice of Hungary. He reached the Second Viennese Arbitrage with the help of Berlin and Rome, and there, however, the surrounding symptoms only proved to him that the Germans were playing a treacherous game. Although he had Foreign Minister Count Csaky sign the three power Anti-Comintern Pact, he refused to participate in the German-Polish war. Upon the initiative of Germany and Italy he concluded a friendship pact with Yugoslavia; even though this had been a long time wish of the Hungarian public, he also knew that by no means through these actions could he prevent the coming turmoil. He did not neglect, at the same time, to make use of his very valuable Anglo-Saxon relationships and connections, and by using his tremendous prestige, he gave detailed information supported by scientific data about his aims and activities to the British Government. Upon the advice of the French diplomat Count De Vienne, he sent a Hungarian politician to the United States. With these measures he wanted to prove the truthfulness and justice of his foreign policy and to secure a greater understanding and corresponding statements. With his illness he was not able to take the excitement of the international situation; thus, when, in contradiction to his previous statements, Hitler declared war on Yugoslavia, and when threats reached him from England, Count Teleki escaped in death. Hungary lost in him a great and iron-willed statesman of immense knowledge and experience.

He was succeeded in the Minister Presidency by the unshakeable and very clever Laszlo Bardossy. Bardossy had been our Ambassador to London and later to Bucharest. After the death of Count Csaky, he obtained the portfolio of Minister of Foreign Affairs in the Teleki Government, but his experiences in the foreign political fields were of rather short duration. As far as his experiences in the internal affairs of the country were concerned, they could be considered nonexistent. He plunged head-first into the tremendous currents moving the entire world in those times; these were currents and factors such as the start of the German-Polish war, the French and British declaration of war on the Third Reich, the sending of Hungarian troops to the Serbian border south of the Danube, and the steps taken by England and the bombing of Hungarian cities. These were followed by such events as the demands which Moscow addressed to Berlin emphasizing her interests in the Balkans, the German troop concentrations on the Soviet Russian border, and on June 22, 1941, Germany's attack on Soviet Russia. These events were followed by the declaration of war on Russia by the Finns, Italians, Rumanians, and the Slovaks. The Japanese delivered a sneak attack on Pearl Harbor, the consequence of which was the declaration of war by the United States on Japan. This was followed by a declaration of war by the Germans and Italians on the United States. In this tremendous burning holocaust which was taking over the rule of the world, the sole aim and task of Bardossy was to try to keep Hungary from drifting into this cataclysm. His efforts were unsuccessful, and on June 27, 1941, he reported to the Houses of Parliament that Hungary had entered into a state of war with Russia; this, of course, was followed by England's declaration of war on Hungary. Acceding to pressure by Germany and Italy, Bardossy declared war also on the United States. Finally in this desperate situation, having no other means left, he tried to resist the ever increasing demands on Hungary by the German military machine for renewed bloody sacrifices. It cannot be considered a diplomatic gesture towards the Western Allies that he had a secret radio transmitter established in the Regent's Palace.

Bardossy was swept out of office probably by some inner political forces, which are yet unknown, and was replaced by Miklos Kallay. Regardless of his political standing, Kallay was received by the public with great doubt and mistrust because his knowledge, experience, and opinions were not thought to meet the requirements of the responsible position of head of the government. Abroad the Germans and the Italians also expressed their mistrust. In neighboring Rumania and Croatia vicious attacking statements were heard. In England Eden made a statement requesting the reconstruction of Czechoslovakia and promised the initiation of such actions to Benes; he also frequently received the Rumanian and Yugoslav politicians. In Slovakia anti-Hungarian feelings were developing. Only the United States, that is to say Washington, manifested sympathy towards Hungary, and stated that the United States did not want to use armed force against her, because under duress she had been forced into the war. In this very precarious atmosphere, Kallay decided to conduct a doublefaced policy. He visited Hitler at his general headquarters stating that there were complaints against Rumania, and he acceded to Hitler's wish to draft 30,000 Hungarian ethnic Germans into SS troops, and to the step-up of food supply shipments to Germany. He visited Pope Pius XII and also Mussolini to whom he spoke of his plans for peace but only received evasive answers in reply. He communicated to Washington that Hungary had started hostile actions against the Russians because they had bombed one of our cities. He wanted to make a friendly gesture towards the Germans with this statement; on the other hand, he refused to declare war against Chile in spite of the strong demands of the Germans. Also he didn't comply to their urging for a settlement of the Jewish question. But he emphasized in the Houses of Parliament that he was going to continue the fight against the Soviets on the side of the Germans. These and similar statements by Kallay were known by the general public and were received with mixed emotions. In the following, I would like to describe those activities of his which remained unknown to the general public but which played in Ankara, Berne, and Lisbon.

A.

The initiater of the negotiations conducted in Ankara was Antal Ullein-Reviczky, head of the press division of the Ministry of Foreign Affairs. Ullein spent his vacation in Spring 1943 on the shores of the Bosphorus at his father-in-law's who was a retired English diplomat. In talking about the Hungarian situation both were of the opinion that the Hungarian Government

96

should send an unofficial and trusted person to Ankara to get in touch with English diplomats and to orient them about the details of the Hungarian question. Kallay sent the trustworthy newspaper man Andras Frey to Ankara, giving him the authority to communicate to competent officials that Hungary was not going to resist against the English and American Armies; that Hungary was ready to turn against the Germans in accordance with a plan that would be worked out in advance by the Allies, and that this proposition was not aimed to preserve their political status but wanted to save the Hungarian nation. The English, receiving these proposals, dwelt lengthily upon them and communicated to Frey through a Hungarian-born English citizen Gyorgy Paloczy-Horvath, who was pretty well-known for his doublefaced activities in Hungary, that it was advisable to send two high ranking Hungarian officers to take up negotiations. This request was discarded by Kallay mostly because of the antipathetic personality of Paloczy-Horvath. Instead, he sent Dezso Ujvary, Hungarian General Consul at Istanbul, to negotiate with the British. He delegated a younger officer of the Ministry of Foreign Affairs, Laszlo Veress, to assist him. The two Hungarian diplomats, after lengthy waits and repeated urgings, finally met with Bennet Sterndàle, Councilor of the British Legation at Ankara, and communicated to him that Hungary was not going to resist to British armed forces if they crossed the Hungarian border, but would turn over immediately all the airfields and railroad lines to them. Also she would accept the orders of the High Command of the Allied Forces, and was ready to take up connections with the same through the radio.

Finally on September 8, 1943, on the yacht of the English Embassy anchored in the Bosphorus, Ujvary and Veress met with Sir Hugh Knachbull-Hughson, the English Ambassador, from whom they received the preliminary conditions according to which: 1. Hungary communicates through official diplomatic channels that she accepts the conditions of the Allies; 2. That this agreement is kept secret until the Allied Armed Forces are about to reach the Hungarian frontier; 3. That Hungary will gradually reduce the number of her armed forces fighting on the side of the Germans; 4. That at the same time she will reduce the economic support granted to the Third Reich; 5. That Hungary will resist if the Germans want to occupy her; 6. That in the given case Hungary will turn over all her resources necessary for the conduct of warfare to the Allies; 7. That Hungary is ready to receive at a given moment the Allied Air Force; 8. That she will establish radio connections with the Allies and that Hungary will not negotiate with anybody else. Veress took these "preliminary conditions" to Budapest in the form of a protocol for ratification where it was received with very mixed emotions. Kallay saw great benevolence in them because they did not request the immediate cessation of hostilities against the Russians, and did not require an immediate attack on the Wehrmacht. On the other hand, some of the other Ministers were of the opinion that the protocol was nothing but a camouflaged demand which repeated the decisions reached by the English-American conference held in Casablanca in January 1943, according to which only one condition was permitted and that was the unconditional surrender. Also the Government was of the unanimous opinion that to accede to the demands of the English would entail an immediate occupation of Hungary by the Germans. Therefore, the formal ratification of the protocol was postponed. The Minister of Interior Ferenc Keresztes-Fischer urged with great emphasis the acceptance of the so-called preliminary conditions and, since the British did not require a signature to this document from Kallay nor from the Minister of Foreign Affairs Ghiczy, they reached a decision to authorize General Consul Ujvary to sign. Baron Wodianer, our Ambassador to Lisbon, notified Sir Reginald Campbell of this fact and with this communication the negotiations of Ankara reached an end.

B.

The secret negotiations conducted at Berne were led by our outstanding and excellent English Ambassador Gyorgy Barcza. Barcza, after having requested his retirement in 1941 for political reasons, had settled down in Switzerland and intended to live there as a private citizen. Nevertheless, he retained his great prestige in Hungarian diplomatic circles. At first Kallay, perhaps because of mistrust, did not want to authorize him to take up negotiations with the British and American foreign representatives stationed in Switzerland. The Minister President was of the opinion that Baron Antal Radvanszky, an official of the Hungarian National Bank, was more suitable for such negotiations since he was able to travel to Switzerland under the pretext of business affairs. Thus he gave orders to Radvanszky to seek contact with Allan Dulles and Royal Taylor, two American diplomats stationed in Berne. Contact was made and the Americans communicated to him that his statements were sent to Washington. Later, upon the urging of former Hungarian Minister President Count Istvan Bethlen, Gyorgy Barcza received authority to negotiate with the English in Switzerland. Barcza traveled immediately to Rome where he obtained an audience with Pope Pius XII and met his old friend Osborne d'Arcy, British Ambassador to the Vatican. He presented a memorandum to Osborne giving details about the Hungarian situation; Osborne, on the other hand, put up the question: "What would be the opinion of Hungary about the creation of a Hungarian-Austrian-Bavarian-Czechoslovakian state federation under the leadership of Archduke Otto Hapsburg?" He promised Barcza that he would send the memorandum immediately to Lisbon, and that he was going to make preparations.

for his negotiations in Switzerland. Barcza traveled from Rome to Montreux, Switzerland, and immediately communicated his arrival to Royal Taylor whom he knew from the time of his stay in Budapest (Author's remark: Taylor was a commissioner of the League of Nations in the Hungarian capital.). He requested the American diplomat to communicate to him all the news which would arrive for him from the Allies.

In May Taylor notified Barcza that a certain "Mr. H." would visit him. At this meeting, which took place at the end of May, Barcza communicated to Mr. H that he was an "English friend-Hungarian," and was living in Montreux as a private citizen but able to get in touch with the Hungarian Minister President Kallay at any time. He also stated that before the Anglo-Saxon powers reach the Hungarian frontier, the Hungarians would not be able to undertake anything because we would be running the risk of immediate occupation by the Germans, and he also emphasized how important it would be that law and order be maintained in Hungary at the end of the war. Finally, he transmitted an Aide Memoire to Mr. H in which he gave details about the policies followed by the country and gave reasons for them. Mr. H promised that he would channel the memorandum to competent authorities and hinted about continuation of the negotiation in the future. These negotiations were renewed and Mr. H communicated that the English acknowledged the fact that the Hungarians could not quit then because of the precarious situation, that they were not thinking of a punitive peace treaty, and they were not opposed to the fact that Horthy and his Government continue the affairs of the country in that transition period. A similar statement was made also by Allen Dulles who represented Washington and who met with Barcza in the middle of July. He added, however, that no territorial promises were made to smaller Allies. [Translator's remarks: He hinted that the Czechs and Rumanians did not receive any promises pertaining to Hungarian territories.]

In July Baron Radvanszky also received a message from Dulles according to which the United States would be willing and ready to negotiate with the former Minister Presidents, either Count Istvan Bethlen or Count Moric Eszterhazy, or eventually with Mr. Lipot Baranyai, the President of the Hungarian National Bank. Barcza and Baron Radvanszky reported the results of their parleys to Kallay who decided to send Baranyai to Switzerland and issued written orders as to the material to be negotiated upon. According to these, Hungary was going to offer any resistance to the Western Allies, and the settlement of territorial questions would be entrusted to the coming peace conference. Baranyai communicated the Hungarian position to Taylor who accepted them as a basis for further negotiations, emphasizing that he was authorized and entrusted by Washington to continue with further negotiation. He also requested that the Hungarian Government authorize one of the Hungarian Ambassadors to continue negotiations with him, and that either Baron Apor at the Vatican, or Velics at Athens, or Baron Bakacs Bessenyei at Vichy would be suitable. Taylor also communicated to Baranyai that the Americans were ready to send a parachute contingency with radio equipment into Hungary. Upon hearing Taylor's communications, Kallay immediately transferred Baron Bakacs Bessenyei to Berne; he also refused to accept a parachute detachment because of its dangerous nature, and instructed Bakacs Bessenyei to conduct negotiations with caution. (This instruction was the reason that Lipot Baranyai refused to participate in further negotiations.) Similar instructions were sent to Barcza pertaining to his negotiations with Mr. H. After these events, the English and Americans changed their attitude and became very rigid. Mr. H and Mr. Taylor demanded that the contingencies of the Hungarian Army be withdrawn from the Russian front, and when Kallay opposed this request and stated that such an action would immediately entail a German occupation of Hungary, they stated that that should be risked.

When the Italians laid down their arms they emphasized their deed as an example to be followed. They also stated that the bombing of Hungarian cities would be unavoidable if the Hungarian industry did not stop delivering to the Third Reich. Both of them urged Kallay to receive an Anglo-Saxon military commission. When they heard in February 1944 that the Hungarians planned to resist on the Carpathian frontier, Mr. H communicated to Barcza that even though he understood the attitude of the Hungarians, it was futile to think of a special handling of Hungary at the peace conferences and that such an event could happen only if Hungary would immediately break relations with the Germans when the Soviet Russian Army reached the Carpathian Mountain Chain. At the same time, Taylor and Dulles notified Bakacs Bessenyei that Washington did not accept the Hungarian-German cooperation against the Russians, but that it was ready to inquire of Moscow whether they would stop at the Hungarian frontier if the Honved Army would not defend it together with the Wehrmacht and if the Hungarians would forbid the German Army to cross their territory, implying the use of force of arms if necessary. Upon receipt of the reports of Barcza and Bakacs Bessenyei, Kallay communicated to them that, since the pressure of the Soviet Russian Army was increasing, we could not break relations with the Germans because the Communist peril would only grow; if he had to choose between the Soviet Russians and the Germans, then of course, one could not decide against the Germans. Taylor and Dulles soon after told Baron Radvanszky, and I quote, "Today the Russians may convince us but we will never convince them." In this matter, the opinion of Mr. H remained unknown. The Berne negotiations ceased, and everything surrounding them; only late in September 1944 did

Bakacs Bessenyei learn, upon request of Miklos Horthy, that he could not negotiate about a Hungarian Armistice without the Soviet Russians.

C.

The trends of the negotiations conducted in Switzerland were in the hands of Baron Alfred Wodianer, Hungarian Ambassador there. In the spring of 1943, Kallay and Count Antal Sigray, a legitimist [Translator's remark: the adherents of the family Hapsburg were called legitimists in Hungary], sent secret messages to him asking him to get in touch with the government in Washington by using the good services of the Hungarian heir to the throne Archduke Otto of Hapsburg. The purpose of his negotiations was to prepare a possible way for Hungary to break relations with the Third Reich and link her fate to that of the Allies. Wodianer communicated this message to Don Jose de Saldanha, a Portugese gentleman who he knew was on very good terms with the Archduke. Saldanha immediately communicated to the Archduke that he wanted to talk to him about a very important matter. The Archduke immediately talked to President Roosevelt, in order to prepare for the arrival of Saldanha arrived in the United States in the beginning of March and communicated the Hungarian message to the Archduke; the Archduke was ready to negotiate with President Roosevelt but first requested further orientation from the Hungarian Government and official authority to conduct negotiations. The meeting between the Archduke and President Roosevelt suffered a delay because the latter was negotiating with Churchill in Quebec. In September and also later in October, Wodianer received letters from Tibor Eckhardt and according to these the Archduke had met with Mr. Roosevelt and also with Mr. Churchill in Quebec; both statesmen were ready and inclined to settle for a conservative solution for Central Europe, but they held it imminently necessary that the Hungarians clarify their relationship with the Allies beforehand. They also seemed ready not to let Hungary fall into the Soviet Union's sphere of interest. Eckhardt also communicated that in Washington there was a favorable attitude towards Hungary. The Archduke sent his brother Archduke Charles Louis to Lisbon and the latter transmitted his messages concerning the parleys and negotiations conducted with President Roosevelt and of the agreement with him. This agreement stipulated that the Allies would guarantee Hungary's independence, that her administration would continue, that her Army would not be disarmed but would be furnished with modern equipment, that her frontiers were to stay the same as those traced in the two Viennese Arbitrage decisions and, concerning the return of the entire Transylvanian territory, a separate proposition would have to be submitted. The conditions of the agreement required a quick and immediate decision by the Hungarian Government. Kallay communicated at the end of November to Wodianer that Archduke Otto may act as Hungarian Head of State only in the case that the Regent abdicate or the Germans occupy the country. He also stated that Hungary was ready to lay down arms to the Western Allies but not to the Soviet Union and requested that the negotiations should not be mentioned in front of Benes who would immediately notify Moscow of their nature. In the autumn months, Wodianer received confidential information from the American Military Attaché, who was on friendly terms with him, according to which Central Europe was a sector which fell into those territories under the Commander in Chief of the Western Allies in Europe, General Eisenhower, and the General wanted to arrive in that territory before the Soviets and did not intend to turn over the Balkans to Soviet rule. Similar communications were received by Wodianer from Kowalsky, a Polish Colonel, who was one of the leading personalities of the Polish resistance movement in London and was oriented about the intentions of General Eisenhower through intimate members of the inner circle. In January 1944, an American citizen of Hungarian origin by the name of Ferenc Deak arrived in Lisbon and communicated to Wodianer that he was the only competent and authorized representative of Washington. He apparently was aware of the negotiations conducted between Archduke Otto and President Roosevelt, but in addition to their results he stated that the Americans wanted to save Hungary from the Soviet Russian sphere of interest and did not wish to have a government similar to that of Mihaly Karolyi; on the contrary, they hoped that Hungary would be the center of the reconstruction of Europe. He also expressed the hope that Hungary's territorial requests be taken favorably and that eventually the return of Transylvania would also be placed on the agenda. Deak added that the only condition was that Hungary should urgently prove through her deeds that she was ready to side with the Allies at any given moment. It would be best if she would withdraw her Armies from the Soviet Russian front and would make communications concerning the situation in Slovakia, Rumania, and the Balkans. Upon receipt of Wodianer's report concerning the communications of Deak, Kallay answered only that the Hungarian Government would gladly withdraw her contingencies from the Soviet Russian front but that she was unable to carry out such actions. In March 1944, Archduke Otto met again with President Roosevelt, and in the course of it, the latter declared that if the Hungarian Government would declare herself ready to support the Allies at any given opportunity, he, the President, would be favorably inclined to make a statement about maintainence of the Transylvanian frontiers of 1940 and towards the settlement of the Czechoslovakian territorial questions by a popular vote. He also authorized the Archduke to transmit this statement to the Hungarian Legation at Lisbon through the secret radio code of the United States. A courier was immediately dispatched from Lisbon to Hungary with the message but, upon hearing of the happenings in Hungary of March 1944, he destroyed the documents and Kallay fled.

I have already given an account in previous parts of this study about the secret negotiations conducted during the Sztojai and Lakatos governments.

While negotiations were being conducted in Ankara, Berne and Lisbon with the knowledge of the Minister President Kallay and with his active participation, we also know of other attempts to negotiate which were started by benevolent but not competent persons, I will give some of the more important ones in the following.

The chief of the press division of the Hungarian Ministry of Foreign Affairs Aladar Szegedi-Masszak worked out a memorandum in the spring of 1943 in which he documented in detail the happenings of the Hungarian foreign policy. He stated that the expansion of Soviet Russia should stop at her 1939 frontiers, that the question of the Danube Valley had to be solved and he proposed an eventual federal solution, that the territorial requests of Hungary in relation to Czechoslovakia and the Transylvanian region should be satisfied, and that if the Croatians wished to return to the Hungarian mother land, they should be permitted this. This memorandum was read by several personalities, probably by Kallay also, and its author sent it to the Hungarian Ambassador at Stockholm, Peter Matuska, with the request that he should transmit the document to the British and American Ambassadors, which he did.

Also in spring 1943, Mr. Gibson, an official of a British trade union, published an article in the *Daily Telegraph,* and according to him, he had had the opportunity to negotiate with Hungarian, Bulgarian, and Rumanian politicians and he had communicated to them the standing of the British Labor Party and that of the British Government. These communications were the following: Hungary was regarded as an adherent of the Axis, that the Hungarian Social Democratic Party and the Press were demanding the return of the Hungarian Army from the Soviet Russian front, and that it was requested that Hungary detach herself from the Third Reich. The communications also stated that it was requested that Hungary return all the territories taken away from Czechoslovakia and other Allies, that Hungary should make it possible for the agricultural problems of Central Europe and the Balkans to be solved, and that she should adhere to that block of countries to which Poland, Czechoslovakia, Yugoslavia, and Greece already adhered. As it turned out, the so-called "Hungarian politician" whom Mr. Gibson negotiated was Vilmos Bohn, former Army Commissar of the Communist Government of Bela Kun, who lived as an emigrant in England. This affair, of course, brought ire and consternation in Hungary.

Ferenc Honthy was the honorary Hungary Consul in Geneva and a member of the Small Holder's Party. An English diplomat advised him to concentrate Hungary's attention on the Soviet Russian Empire because Hungary's fate would be decided by her. Honthy got in touch with a Soviet Russian personality who formerly had held a high position in the Russian diplomatic corps. This unknown personage communicated to Honthy that the primary task of the Allies was to annihilate the German armed forces, and the Soviet Union had a leading role in this action; therefore, all demands of Moscow in the peace negotiations and pacts were going to be satisfied to the very last. The Soviet Russians were going to demand the Baltic states, Bessarabia, and those territories of Poland which were not inhabited by ethnic Poles; the fate of Carpatho-Ruthenia in Hungary depended on the peace guarantees given by the Hungarians to the Soviet Russians, for the Russian Empire did not want to expand her frontier and was ready to accept ethnic views but demanded a guarantee. Hungary had made some great mistakes in the past but the future was more important; therefore, it seemed advisable that the Hungarian Government immediately withdraw her troops from the Eastern Front and break relationship with the Third Reich. Eventual dangerous consequences of such actions would be prevented if Hungary would let Anglo-Saxon parachutists descend in her territories, and later Transylvania would gain autonomy. Honthy made personal report of these meetings to the Hungarian Ministry of Foreign Affairs. There, however, they communicated to him that closer contact with the Soviet Russians would be opposed by the Regent and nobody would take the responsibility of such a step.

Janos Marty, intelligence officer of the Hungarian Consulate Service and born in Vienna, was assigned the mission to halt the armed partisan activities of the Tito followers on Hungarian territory. Marty met several times with Tito at the frontier railroad station Gyekenyes and then agreed mutually not to attack each other, and in case the British did occupy the Balkans, Tito would join them and would stop at the Hungarian frontiers leaving Hungary to the English. As we have seen, this agreement had some very tragic consequences on October 15, 1944.

Chapter III
ATTEMPTS TO FORM EXILE GOVERNMENTS

Count Michel de Vienne was the French Ambassador to Budapest during the Thirties. He was a descendant of an ancient French aristocratic family, and he established many friendly relationships in Budapest due to his excellent manners and outstanding spiritual wit. He frequently contacted the leading political personalities of Hungary and established a very friendly and intimate relation with Gyula Gombos and with his Minister of Foreign Affairs Kalman Kanya.

In the spring of 1940, Count de Vienne came to Budapest as a private citizen and got in touch with the Minister President of that time, Count Pal Teleki; he advised Teleki that in case of a crisis he should influence the Regent to leave Hungary and to form an exile government somewhere in the West which would be accepted by the major powers of the world. Such an exile government would clearly prove the antipathy of Hungary towards the Third Reich whatever happened later. In the spirit of ancient maritime laws which say no captain may leave the sinking ship and also as a Hungarian gentleman and soldier listening to his innermost voice of honor, the Regent did not even want to consider the proposition and advice of Count de Vienne. The Minister President, however, not wanting to lose such an opportunity and desiring to answer the friendly gesture of the Anglo-Saxon powers, wanted to initiate some action, and decided that he would send Tibor Eckhardt, a representative in Parliament and President of the Small Holder's Party, to Washington D.C. Count Teleki wanted to solve two problems with this move. On one hand, he would be able to place an excellent politician accustomed to dealing with foreign political representatives in a position of trust and importance; on the other hand, he would have eliminated the ever disagreeable presence of a member of the Houses of Parliament who in the past twenty years through his whims and sometimes irresponsible attitude had created much trouble in the internal and foreign political sphere for the Government.

Eckhardt accepted this mission but the final details were not easy ones. Eckhardt needed permission for a leave of absence from the House of Commons to be able to go abroad, plus his mission could not be kept secret and it was subject to vehement attacks by the extreme right wing (National Socialist) party. Furthermore, Eckhardt also needed money and to transfer funds to Washington involved technical difficulties. Nevertheless, the House of Commons voted and granted him a furlough and Lipot Baranyai, president of the Hungarian National Bank, saw to it that one million dollars was transferred to the Hungarian Embassy in Washington to be disposed of exclusively by Regent Horthy, Minister President Teleki, and Baranyai himself.

Eckhardt's travels suffered delays because the English Government dragged out the granting of a transit visa. Finally Eckhardt traveled through Egypt to Washington and immediately got in touch with the Hungarian circles representing various political opinions and factions in the United States. His actions in connection with Archduke Otto, Hungarian heir to the throne, became very well known but he by no means fulfilled the expectations balancing on his stay in the United States.

Sir Owen O'Malley, British Ambassador to Budapest, also brought to the attention of the Regent at the beginning of the year 1940 the great danger which would be created if Hungary acceded to the wishes of the Third Reich to transit the country. In his answer, the Regent emphasized that he would never accede to such wishes, but that he would react immediately instead by abdicating and forming an exile government abroad in order to give a constitutional emphasis to his opposition to such action. At that time the Regent sought to entrust the formation of an exile government to Count Istvan Bethlen. O'Malley reported this conversation to his government.

At the same time Gyorgy Barcza, Hungarian Ambassador to London, upon his own initiative and assuming the responsibility, put the question to Sir Alexander Cadogan, Under Secretary of the British Foreign Office, about the stand of the Government of Britain should Horthy and his government transfer their seat to England. Cadogan answered that, "the British Royal Government would be highly honored, would be very pleased and would recognize the Hungarian Government."

The Hungarian Government acknowledged these British statements and inquired whether the British Government would recognize such a Hungarian exile government as the constitutional representative of the country whatever happened in the future. The Hungarian Government did not get an answer to this question, but O'Malley did inquire as to the carrying out of such a plan on the eve of the attack planned by the Third Reich against Yugoslavia. He received an evasive answer. The reason for this hesitant attitude was that Teleki was afraid that Edward Benes, who had mighty patrons in London, would be able to halt the recognition of the Hungarian exile government by the British Government. After Teleki's suicide, O'Malley visited the Regent and received the information that Hungary was going to participate in the German-Yugoslav conflict (like I described above) for the reasons that Hungary had historical connections with Germany, that she needed a road to the sea, that she wanted to gain back her lost territories, that she could not expect any help from the British, and last but not least, that the Third Reich might take vengeance on Hungary. Horthy stated at the time that the formation of an exile government could not be taken into consideration at the moment. O'Malley enumerated important arguments and also made bitter reproaches to the Regent who answered, "It is all in vain, my decision is firm."

On April 7, 1940, the British Government ceased diplomatic relations with Hungary, and the English flyers bombed the cities of Pecs, Szeged, and Villany.

According to Ambassador Barcza, Churchill made the following statement: "The Hungarian Government is in the right. We English have made mistakes in the past. Hungary always stated openly that she wanted to reacquire those territories that were taken away from her, and it is humanly comprehensible that her armies are occupying those. I am sorry that politically I cannot do anything else but break diplomatic relations with you."

Gyorgy Barcza, one of the most outstanding of our five excellent diplomats abroad, was called back by our Government from London and he requested his immediate retirement. Later (as we already saw above) he continued to contribute with outstanding service to his country.

In 1943, members of our diplomatic corps abroad observing the hesitant and inadequate attitudes of the Kallay Government and the futile developments of the situation on the war front realized that their efforts were also slowly becoming meaningless. At this time, upon initiative of former Ambassadors Gyorgy Barcza and Gyorgy Bakacs-Bessenyei, these diplomats started to organize into a group by the name of the Dissidents. Baron Apor, Baron Wodianer, Chika, Ullein, Pelenyi, and many others joined this organization. The British and American Governments communicated their benevolence and pleasure to Barcza. Shortly before the fateful day of March 19, 1944, the Hungarian Government sought to support this organization and sent thirty-five kilograms of gold through the Hungarian National Bank to be deposited with the Swiss National Bank in the trust of Bakacs-Bessenyei, Baron Radvanszky, and Vladar. (Writer's remark: this fund was also called later the "Horthy Fund" without any particular foundation.)

The Dissident diplomats never formed an exile government and this gold later became the subject of heated, bitter and disagreeable arguments.

Chapter IV

THE ATTITUDE OF THE ETHNIC GERMANS
IN HUNGARY

I remind the reader that the pages of Hungarian history know three phases of the settlement of Germans in Hungary.

First, already our kings of the family Arpad settled into the foothills of the Northern Carpathian Mountains; in the Szepesseg area, Zipsers of Flemish origin; and into the foothills of the Southern Carpathian Mountains, in the area known as Barczag, Germans or so-called "Saxons" coming from various parts of Germany. The first settlers, the Zipsers, for about 800 years gave outstanding artisans, merchants, noted artists, scientists, and soldiers to Hungary. (Author's remark: among them, for instance, one of the most outstanding generals of the fight for liberty in 1848-49, General Arthur Gorgey.) The second ones, the Saxons, however, standing on the protection of the rights granted to them by certain royal decrees, opposed the Hungarian national interests for the most part, even after Francis Joseph I rescinded their ancient privileges.

The second phase of settlement is the one that was initiated by the Viennese Government after the cessation of Turkish occupation; the Turkish era of devastation which left vast territories uninhabited and uncultivated in southern Hungary, in Transdanubia, and in the area surrounding the capital city. In these uninhabited areas the Austrian Government settled several hundred thousand Germans from the Schwarzwald (the Black Forest), from the Rhine bank, and from Alsace. These farmers and artisans worked and toiled in the most fertile areas of the country and gave very valuable services to their land through their skill, their participation in public administration and the army; however, there never was an opportunity which would subject their loyalty to the test. They remained neutral during the war for liberty in 1848-49.

The third phase or category is that in which German settlers slowly drifted into Hungary from the neighboring Tyrolean, Carinthian, and Styrian regions of Austria. They were usually called "Schwabians" (or as the Hungarians spell it "Svab") but they also had local names which varied with the area. For instance, the "Ponzichter" lived in the area of Sopron because they liked to grow beans. The name of those living in the area of Pozsony (at present the Czech Bratislava), were called the "Kraxlhuber" because they mounted every Sunday to their high vineyards. The German artisans of the country of Zemplen were called the "Wanderbursch" because in their apprentice years they went wandering. The Germans of the Baranya county area were called the "Weinpeisser" because they bite their red wine while tasting it, so it was said. These drifters were laboring people; they always stayed uninterested and strange to the affairs of Hungary and the Hungarian Nation with the exception of those in the Pozsony area who always participated in all the Hungarian events. Pozsony was for centuries the crowning city and also the seat of the Hungarian Parliament.

The nationalistic idea, which was born and which developed in the 19th century, had aspirants and followers also among the Schwabs of Hungary. In Hungary, like everywhere else in the world, they were led by personalities, who either did it because of their idealistic tendencies or because they just wanted to be in the limelight; the leaders began to cause disagreeable moments for the various governments and administrative organs of all countries including Hungary. Since the support for these movements did not come from Germany or from Austria, they remained an internal affair of Hungary and were treated more or less benevolently by Hungarian authorities, but it has to be emphasized that it did not have a great response among the ethnic circles. They remained hard working citizens of their country, served as soldiers, public servants, and even willingly and gladly changed their names to Hungarian ones.

This peaceful coexistence remained undisturbed until the atmosphere of the Hitlerian era struck and in a few years changed everything radically.

According to the 1920 census data, there were 551,600 ethnic Germans living within the Hungarian limits as set by the Treaty of Trianon. Under the leadership of Transylvanian Saxon Dr. Gustav Gratz and the executive management of Parliamentary Deputy Dr. Jakab Bleyer, there was formed in 1924 the "Ungarlandisch-Deutcher Volksbildungsverein." [Translated: German-Hungarian People's Educational Association] (U.D.V.) This organization first worked in the interest of developing a German-Hungarian understanding, and insisted upon the revisions of the peace treaty; until it fell into the clutches of the press of the Third Reich in the early 1930's, it also promoted culture and professional knowledge. The German press at that time wrote about the oppression which the ethnic Germans were being subjected to in Hungary, and the U.D.V. stepped onto the scene with demands which created uneasiness in the Hungarian political circles; at this point Gyula Gombos, Minister President at the time and of outstanding political loyalty and equipoise, started to find mutual solutions with Dr. Jakab Steinacker, the director of the "Volksbund der Auslanddeutschen" (V.B.A.) [Translated: Association of the German People Living Abroad] on one of his visits to Germany.

This man enlightened him about Hitler's opinions; according to Hitler there was no difference between Germans of the Reich and those living abroad, and they both have to serve the cause of Germany. He encouraged Gratz to continue his work in the U.D.V., but also said that there was going to be another more militant organization founded in Hungary in the future. This organization was the "Volksdeutsche Kameradschaft" [in English: Ethnic German Collegiate Society] which was founded in 1934 and managed by Ferenc Basch who also had very strong connections with the German secret organization "Ausslandsdienst." [Translated: Foreign Service Organization] He also received orders from the same.

From then on the German minority became restless, their voice became sharp and their paper, the *Deutscher Volksbote* [Translated: German Popular Messenger], published attacking articles which immediately were echoed in the papers of the Third Reich; in those times we could read in such papers that, and I quote: "The German frontier is at the Lake of Balaton; we cannot be satisfied to have only the Burgenland, for the German cultural sphere is equal to German territory." The Hungarian courts sentenced to prison some of these agents and instigators, and Foreign Minister Kanya directed the attention of German Foreign Minister Baron Karl Neurath to these Pan-Germanic intrigues during the latter's visit to Budapest in September 1936. But there were other rather grave symptoms appearing also. Those were, for instance, that the youth organization called "Wander-vögel" [Translated: Migrating Birds] started to drift into Hungary from Germany; they distributed handbills, newspaper clippings and scrapbooks which all propagated National Socialist and anti-Semitic ideas. They also propagated that the Hungarian ethnic Germans should form a "Volksgruppe" [Translated: Ethnic group] and the result of this instigation was that news was spread stating that Hitler would cut as much as he wanted out of Hungarian territory. All this, of course, resulted in a growing mistrust and antipathy among the Hungarians for the propagandistic Germans; even our own Schwabs were opposed to these.

After the Austrian Anschluss, the "Volksdeutsche Mittelstelle" [Translated: Ethnic German Central Office] seated in Berlin whose task it was to spread the political philosophy of the Third Reich, opened a new central office in Vienna under the leadership of Dr. Wilhelm Höttl and was supported with ample funds. This office was responsible for the area of Italy and East Central Europe. Of course, Hottl immediately got in touch with the right wing elements in Hungary, he also somehow enticed into his services the Hungarian newspaper *Magyarság*, and he established channels for German money to drift into Hungary. His influence in Hungarian internal affairs through his secret and well-organized channels, both in political and economic affairs, was soon perceptible. In the Hottl's intrigues, the members of the U.D.V. acted as spies and denunciators, and they had ample and outstanding results.

The Teleki government disbanded the U.D.V. in 1940 and permitted instead the organization of the "Volksbund der Deutschen in Ungarn." [Translated: People's Association of Germans in Hungary] The Government also permitted further appearance of the paper *Deutscher Volksbot.* [Translated: German People's Messenger]. This organization was under the leadership of the disagreeable, argumentative, and hateful person, Dr. Ferenc Basch, who instigated the Hungarian ethnic Germans in every way in spite of their outstanding and eminent position in all phases and walks of Hungarian life: the ethnic Germans of Hungary, who had had unlimited privileges and unlimited possibilities for development, changed almost overnight to an egocentric, grasping and demanding force in the country. At the end of the Thirties the Hungarian ethnic Germans refused to accede to the regulations of the Hungarian authorities, refused to pay taxes, refused to enter military services, refused to speak the Hungarian language, and upon every question put to them in Hungarian, they answered rudely and assumed a threatening attitude. They gladly accepted service in the SS ranks upon summons issued by the Third Reich, and they gladly "escaped," as they called it, to Germany giving up their work, their farms and everything. The Volksbund promoted and encouraged the idea that the southern Hungarian territories returned to the mother country after the German-Yugoslav conflict should be called the "Schwabische Turkei" [Translated: Schwabian Turkey] or "Prinz Eugen Gau" [Prince Eugene Administrative District] and they should be annexed. According to these demands the cities of Eszek, Pecs, Temesvar, and Orsova, their respective regions, plus the county of Tolna, and the mining districts of Transylvania should become a separate Gau, administrative district, outside Germany but under the authority of the Third Reich.

This idea is still alive in certain Austrian circles and can be illustrated by the small map attached which was edited in the Fifties in Vienna. The only difference is that the Burgenland (Author's remark: which always was ethnographically, historically Hungarian) is shown three times as large as it actually is, and they do not show the Schwabische Turkei which comprises the Southern Hungarian Bacska and which at present belongs to Yugoslavia.

What may have been Adolf Hitler's ideas about Hungary and her fate in case the Third Reich would have won the war, General Bela Vasvary, former commanding general of the 16th Hungarian Division, related to me in 1949 as follows.

In 1946, he (General Vasvary) with several other Hungarian refugees in the Austrian Carinthia, in the English Zone, invited all Hungarians for a little Christmas celebration. In this refugee

111

camp lived also Emil Kovarc, a notorious, bloodthirsty adherent of Ferenc Szalasi. He (Kovarc) was not invited; he was awaiting his extradition to the Communist Hungarian authorities. Finally the good hearted Hungarians invited him also out of pity; knowing that he had spent a long time in the Third Reich, Vasvary asked whether he knew what Hitler would have done with Hungary in case of a victory. Emil Kovarc, being well informed, stated that Hitler had wanted to change Hungary into a protectorate state in which he would have left constitutional institutions, the Parliament, a responsible Government, the courts and its administrative organization; however, all positions of responsibility in the Government, in the judicial, in the public administration, in the finances and also in the counties would have been filled with Germans from the Third Reich or absolutely trustworthy, ethnic Germans from Hungary. In the Parliament he would have introduced a one-party system.

With this I think the picture is complete.